For the Newman Family—
Happy Cooking &
Happy Eating. Awful picture of me
the grilling book is much better

Love Eileen 2004

food network kitchens

making it
easy

Meredith® Books
Des Moines, Iowa

Food Network Kitchens
Making It Easy

Editor: Jennifer Dorland Darling
Contributing Editor: Lisa Kingsley
Contributing Writers: Sharon Glassman,
Raquel Pelzel
Senior Associate Design Director: Mick Schnepf
Graphic Designer: Joline Rivera, idesign&associates, inc.
Copy Chief: Terri Fredrickson
Publishing Operations Manager: Karen Schirm
Managers, Book Production: Pam Kvitne, Marjorie J.
Schenkelberg, Rick von Holdt, Mark Weaver
Edit and Design Production Coordinator: Mary Lee Gavin
Editorial Assistant: Cheryl Eckert
Contributing Copy Editor: Joyce Gemperlein
Contributing Proofreaders: Maria Duryée, Gretchen Kauffman,
Elise Marton
Photographers: Mark Ferri, Robert Jacobs
Recipe Editor: Shelli McConnell
Prop Stylist: Francine Matalon-Degni
Indexer: Elizabeth Parson

Meredith® Books
Editor in Chief: Linda Raglan Cunningham
Design Director: Matt Strelecki
Managing Editor: Gregory H. Kayko

Publisher: James D. Blume
Executive Director, Marketing: Jeffrey Myers
Executive Director, New Business Development: Todd M. Davis
Executive Director, Sales: Ken Zagor
Director, Operations: George A. Susral
Director, Production: Douglas M. Johnston
Business Director: Jim Leonard
Vice President and General Manager: Douglas J. Guendel

Meredith Publishing Group
President, Publishing Group: Stephen M. Lacy
Vice President-Publishing Director: Bob Mate

Meredith Corporation
Chairman and Chief Executive Officer: William T. Kerr

In Memoriam: E.T. Meredith III (1933-2003)

Pictured on front cover: Tortilla Soup
(see recipe, page 36)

Our second cookbook really hits home for everyone here at Food Network Kitchens. Like you, we're all pressed for time these days. But we don't want to miss out on any opportunity to gather around the table with those we love for a great home-cooked meal.

Making It Easy is filled with real-life recipes and tips from our staff to get you inspired and keep things simple at the same time. While our incredible Food Network Kitchens team—at right—inspired this book, I want to give special thanks to a few people.

First, thanks to our development team headed up by Test Kitchen Director Katherine Alford. Juggling her day between work and being Abigail's mom made her a natural for this book. Our recipe developers Suki Hertz, Santos Loo, Mory Thomas, and Vivian Jao perfected each recipe to guarantee ease and success every time. Thanks also to recipe editor Miriam Garron and our super-shopper Stacy Meyer.

Our own Fab Five in the photo studio deserve kudos too: Food stylists Krista Ruane and Mory Thomas, photographers Mark Ferri and Robert Jacobs, and stylist Francine Matalon-Degni created these gorgeous food shots.

Look for the Food Network Kitchens traveling team that performs cooking demos all over the country. A big thanks to Susan Maynard for all the travel arrangements.

Finally to everyone here at Scripps Networks for their unflagging support and encouragement—especially our president Judy Girard, marketing vice president Adam Rockmore, and his team Mark O'Connor and Carrie Welch. And to the team at Meredith: editors Jennifer Darling and Lisa Kingsley and creative team Mick Schnepf and Joline Rivera—thanks for your insights and design.

We hope we've succeeded in *Making It Easy*—for you. Enjoy every bite!

Susan Stockton
Vice President, Culinary Production
Food Network

who's who

Top row, left to right: Stacey Meyer, Katherine Alford, Miriam Garron, Suki Hertz, Bob Hoebee, David Martin
Second row, left to right: Rob Bleifer, Jill Novatt, Eileen McClash, Lissa Wood, Jay Brooks, Susan Maynard
Third row, left to right: Mory Thomas, Susan Stockton, Athen Fleming, Jonathan Milder, Derek Flynn, Lynn Kearney
Bottom row, left to right: Andrea Steinberg, Miguel DeLeon, Santos Loo, Krista Ruane, Harriet Siew

We're the Kitchen behind the TV kitchens you see on your favorite Food Network shows. And we're passionate about food. We are shoppers, cooks, food stylists, testers and tasters, recipe developers, caterers, editors, and food researchers. We make sure every dish you see on air looks gorgeous and tastes great. And we have a great time doing it! If we've learned anything in more than a decade of cooking behind the scenes for Food Network, it's how to make shopping, prep, cooking, and cleanup as quick and easy as possible. Now we get to share our tips with you.

contents

Did you know that:

You have baby cheesecakes in your pantry? Your pressure cooker makes risotto? You can create a fruit tart in 30 minutes? Your microwave does more than pop corn? There's a one-pot Caribbean feast in your pressure cooker?

And, shhh, don't tell your *nonna* you used a slow cooker to make that fabulous Sunday gravy.

That's right. We're *Making It Easy*. It's our mantra in Food Network Kitchens.

Whether it's a simple meal or dinner for guests, we've got recipes that will get you there.

We know you have busy lives because you've told us—and we do too. We cook up amazing foods for our cooking shows all day long: hundreds of recipes from celebrity chefs, cookbook authors, and home cooks—cuisine from New York to New Delhi. Then we go home and cook for our families.

Don't get us wrong. We love it. We're planning our next meal during our present meal. But, like you, we want to sit down to something fresh, delicious, and comforting at the end of the day—and we want to make quick work of it!

So we put our heads together and came up with our best strategies to get food on the table with minimum effort and huge applause. Look for one of the following icons at the top of each page. Every recipe in this book utilizes one of these four strategies.

• **PANTRY PICKS:** Make the most of what's in your cupboards, fridge, and freezer. Check out "Stock Your Pantry" on page 214 and forget those last minute trips to the store.

• **DOUBLE DUTY:** Cook once, eat twice. The only things you'll have left over are the makings of tomorrow's great meals.

Whether it's your dream kitchen or your first kitchen, we have lots of ideas for setting up pantries and tons of tips for making cooking a breeze:

• **REAL QUICK:** You'll get most of these recipes on the table in 30 minutes or less.

• **COOL TOOLS:** Dust off that slow cooker, microwave, and pressure cooker. We've got some new twists on old appliances.

Use the **Game Plan** at the top of recipes for great tips on how to make the most of your cooking time.

ShopSmart tips guide you quickly through the grocery store, and **Know-How** tips will have you cooking like a pro.

Even if you're pressed for time, you've got time to eat—and eat very well—something you've cooked yourself. So dig in!

Look for this symbol to find quick-to-cook recipes that are big on flavor.

- ● pantry picks
- ● double duty
- ● **real quick**
- ● cool tools

A DELICIOUS MEAL IN NO TIME? SURE THING! NOT ONLY ARE THESE RECIPES EASY TO PREPARE, BUT THEY'RE ALSO FOOD NETWORK KITCHENS FLAVORFUL.

1. COOK SIMPLE. A few simply cooked, well-chosen ingredients can create a wonderful, boldly flavored meal that's memorable, quick, and easy. A few shortcut combinations worth trying? Lemon zest in rice or a swirl of chile in chicken soup. Check out these recipes: Bowties with Cauliflower, Olives & Lemon (page 67), and Tortilla Soup (page 36).

2. SHOP SMART. Cutting down on prep time by buying prepared fresh foods is a powerful way to increase kitchen comfort. Your supermarket and local salad bar are great sources for time-savers, such as cooked vegetables and roasted chickens, that are perfectly suited to the recipes in this book. Buying individually portioned cuts of meat and fish is another way to minimize prep time. For added flavor, buy jarred roasted peppers, pesto, and spreads to use as condiments and seasonings.

3. BUY SEASONAL; BUY LOCAL. Local food is a staple of many top restaurants; cooking with it is a simple way to better the taste of home-prepared foods. Pears in the Northeast in fall, summer corn in the Midwest, and California avocados in spring are just a few examples of foods that offer a head start to natural good taste.

4. GAME PLAN IT. Get the most done in the least amount of time by planning ahead. Take a minute before you cook to get your tools in place. Take one more minute to identify the simplest ways to prepare your ingredients. "Diced" garlic can be more quickly smashed with the side of a knife blade. Smash potatoes with the peels on; they taste great and look cool too. Take advantage of cooking time to toss a salad or set the table.

5. MIX AND MATCH. You don't have to make everything from scratch for a meal to offer home-cooked comfort—and you don't have to do everything yourself. The right balance of homemade and store-bought reduces cooking time while keeping fresh flavors and fun at their peak. Serve our spicy Tortilla Soup (page 36) followed by Chicken with Tomatoes & Pepperoncini (page 103), a loaf of crusty store-bought bread, and a salad of premixed greens. Set out sundae fixings for dessert. Invite housemates, friends, and family to pour the wine, toss the salad, or chat with you in the kitchen.

6. SERVE BIG AND BOLD. Simple food simply served makes for meals filled with flavor and good feeling. Family-style meals served on colorful platters, in bowls—even on a cutting board—make guests feel warm and cozy as they break bread together. Feel free to mix and match plates and serving pieces, or serve on one solid hue that sets off the foods' natural colors.

Look for this symbol to pinpoint recipes that make the most of what you have on hand.

● **pantry picks**
● ~~double duty~~
○ ~~...~~
○ ~~...~~

WHEN IT COMES TO FRESH, FLAVORFUL COMFORT FOODS, SOME OF TODAY'S BEST DISHES ARE COMING OUT OF THE CLOSET, THE FRIDGE, AND THE LARDER. WITH A FEW BASIC INGREDIENTS, EVEN THE MOST OCCASIONAL CHEF CAN TURN BASICS INTO SATISFYING THAI SHRIMP CURRY, COZY COCONUT-LIME PUDDING CAKES, OR PERFECT PANINI. HERE'S HOW:

1. STOCK UP. One of the most comforting things about a well-stocked kitchen is knowing you have your staples on hand. Keep a list of these items in your computer or PDA so you don't have to rewrite your core shopping list each time you need it. Shop for all your dry goods (flour, sugar, etc.) at one time—monthly. Replenish lemons, eggs, butter, and long-lasting refrigerated supplies biweekly. Then you can purchase fresh foods in the express line!

2. MAXIMIZE MULTITASKERS. Spice and herb blends, seasoned vinegars, and the jarred olive pastes known as tapenades can add flavor to different dishes in multiple wonderful ways. Keep a selection in your pantry to create new dishes from old favorites.

3. ORGANIZE IN A FLASH. The bad news: You won't use it if you can't see it. The good news: Making ingredients visible takes a lot less time than looking for them! Cluster similar ethnic ingredients in one place so you can find them fast. Put kids' snacks at eye level so you know when it's time to stock up. Transfer cereals, rice, and baking supplies to clear, labeled, resealable containers so you can grab what you're looking for that much easier.

4. PANTRIFY YOUR FRIDGE. They don't last forever, but carrots, celery, cheeses, and eggs are durable refrigerator basics that can be turned into zillions of great dishes. To keep ingredients fresh longer, store vegetables in one crisper and fruits in another. Place strong cheeses away from mild-tasting butter, and be sure to wrap cured or smoked meats securely to keep them fresh and insulated from more delicate foods. Check your condiments at least every six months. Toss the ones that have lost their kick, then add them to your next shopping list.

5. BE FREEZER-FRIENDLY. Wrap, label, and date all items before placing them in the freezer. When it comes to freezing, brothy soups, stews, and non cream-based sauces do better than raw fish, creamy soups, or delicate vegetables. Shorten the cooking time of frozen meats and poultry by quick-thawing them in the microwave. Second choice? Place meats and poultry into a plastic bag and thaw them in a bowl of cool running water—great for defrosting shrimp too. Never leave frozen foods to thaw on the counter.

Look for this symbol to zero in on recipes that take advantage of kitchen gadgetry both old and new.

● pantry picks
● double duty
● real quick
● **cool tools**

FOOD NETWORK KITCHENS HAS ASSEMBLED A LIST OF THE MOST VERSATILE KITCHEN TOOLS ON THE PLANET. THESE ARE THE ONES WE USE IN OUR HOME KITCHENS TO MAKE COOKING EASIER, WHETHER WE'RE BLENDING INGREDIENTS FOR A SNAPPY STIR-FRY OR PUTTING A SLOW COOKER TO NEW USE. CHECK OUT OUR DISCOVERIES AND YOU MAY FIND THAT SOME OF TODAY'S "NEWEST" TOOLS AWAIT YOU IN YOUR KITCHEN, BASEMENT, OR ATTIC.

1. POWERFUL MINITOOLS: Plug in a blender or minichopper to turn whole foods into "diced" ingredients that let you get to the fun part of cooking more quickly.

2. MICROWAVES AND PRESSURE COOKERS* ARE TIME-SAVERS: Shorten the stretch from start to finish by tapping cookers that get the job done deliciously fast. Microwaves cook quickly with minimal cleanup. Pressure cookers, which use the power of intense steam, can make a lamb curry in one-third the time of your stove top.

3. SLOW COOKERS* ARE FLAVOR BOOSTERS: To boost the flavors of today's comfort cooking, we've rediscovered the slow cooker, a star of the '70s that can produce modern stews and soups while you're out for the day. Brown meats and veggies before slow cooking to increase their flavor.

*See page 218-219 for details about slow cookers and pressure cookers.

4. SAFETY: A key rule of cooking: Food's no fun if it's burned and can be very dangerous if it's on fire! Keep your kitchen fire extinguisher within reach of your cooking area and check it annually to make sure it's up-to-date.

Less dramatic, daily safety practices are also vitally important to kitchen safety. Wash your hands with soap and warm water before beginning any recipe to remove germs from your ingredients list. Wash your hands again after handling chicken, and remove germy residues from plastic cutting boards by washing them in your dishwasher on the "sanitizer" cycle. The dishwasher is also a great place to sterilize kitchen sponges.

An essential kitchen tool? An instant-read thermometer. Use it to check on the cooking status of meats so they're well cooked but not overcooked. Stock the drawer closest to your stove with colorful pot holders and trivets to make safety look even better.

5. FUN FLAVORS: Seasonings are comfort-food tools that you can put to use in myriad ways in the same manner a painter applies shades of color to a canvas. Adding soy sauce, dried mushrooms, or orange zest is a great way to heighten the flavors of stews and salads. Fresh herbs and grated cheeses highlight the flavors of soups and nibbles.

Look for this symbol to locate recipes that give you a head start on dinner. Cook once, eat twice.

● pantry picks

● **double duty**

○ real quick

○ cool tools

PRECOOKED INGREDIENTS ARE THE BUILDING BLOCKS OF MANY GREAT MEALS, WHETHER YOU BUY THEM IN YOUR LOCAL SUPERMARKET OR FIND THEM LEFT OVER FROM LAST NIGHT'S TAKEOUT. COOKING CAN BE TWICE AS FUN WHEN EVERYTHING YOU PREPARE HAS MULTIPLE USES. HERE ARE A FEW TIME-SAVING, FUN-BOOSTING, TWO-FOR-ONES WE DISCOVERED IN FOOD NETWORK KITCHENS.

I. CHOP PLUS ONE: While you're cutting onions, garlic, scallions, or herbs for today's meal, chop a little extra to use tomorrow. Ingredients such as these can stay fresh for up to four days if stored in sealed containers. Do the same thing when grating cheese. Keep the surplus fresh by storing it in a sealed container in your fridge, where it will keep for up to a week.

2. FUTURE FOUNDATIONS: Cook double portions of starches tonight and you'll have the building blocks for great meals tomorrow. Leftover bread makes great Summer Tomato Bread Salad with Scallops (page 42); extra rice is perfect for Thai Shrimp & Rice Soup (page 31). Combine a protein, a cheese, and a fruit to make a delicious, impromptu salad.

3. MULTITASK IT: Making pesto or other sauces? Hold on to the extra to use as sandwich spreads and condiments for meals to come. Freeze to reuse as needed. One fun example: Tunisian Pesto (page 14) made as a dip for shrimp works wonderfully when stirred into chicken soup.

4. THINK BIG: The Sunday night meal is a great source of double-duty lunches and dinners throughout the week. Roast a turkey and you'll have enough leftovers for Turkey Hoppin' John (page 127), Turkey Enchilada Casserole (page 126), and Turkey Turnovers (page 128).

5. SHAMELESS SERVING: Some folks turn their noses up at leftovers, no matter how great they taste—so don't tell 'em! Serve double-duty dishes in your finest bowls and on your best platters. What diners don't know won't hurt their taste buds. In fact, they'll love it.

citrus-spiced mixed olives • tuscan bean dip • grilled shrimp cocktail • tunisian pesto • fresh green chutney • wasabi guacamole • blasted balsamic chicken wings • goat cheese nut log with chile • fig & almond tart • pork satay • artichoke, potato & chorizo tortilla • fresh cheese quesadillas with arugula & radish

getting
started

Our first tastes put the fun and exciting into fast and easy. Throw together bold small plates for company or for yourself.

citrus-spiced mixed olives
2 cups

3 tablespoons olive oil

2 cloves garlic, smashed

1½ teaspoons crushed red pepper

1 large sprig fresh rosemary,
2 bay leaves, or both

Zest of 1 orange, peeled in long strips with a vegetable peeler

Zest of 1 lemon, peeled in long strips with a vegetable peeler

12 ounces mixed olives, such as kalamata, niçoise, or cerignola, drained

½ teaspoon kosher salt

Freshly ground black pepper

Put the olive oil, garlic, red pepper, herbs, and citrus zests in a medium skillet. Heat over medium-high heat, swirling the pan until the mixture is fragrant, 3 to 4 minutes. Add the olives, salt, and pepper and cook, stirring occasionally, until the garlic is golden and the zest begins to curl, about 5 minutes more. Discard and remove bay leaves, if using. Serve warm or at room temperature.

Glossy, plump, and gorgeous, our Citrus-Spiced Mixed Olives are primo party starters. Toss 'em together, then leave them out while you mingle with your guests.

tuscan bean dip
4 servings

1 small baguette, thinly sliced

4 cloves garlic

1½ teaspoons kosher salt, plus additional for seasoning

¼ cup extra-virgin olive oil

2 sprigs fresh rosemary, leaves stripped (about 1½ tablespoons)

Pinch crushed red pepper

1 15-ounce can cannellini beans, rinsed and drained

Crisp vegetables, for dipping (optional)

1. Preheat oven to 400°F. Lay bread on a baking sheet. Rub each slice with a clove of garlic and sprinkle with a pinch of salt; reserve garlic clove. Toast in oven until golden, about 8 minutes.

2. Chop all garlic cloves. Cook garlic in the olive oil in a small skillet over medium-high heat, stirring, until it is golden, about 3 minutes. Pull skillet from heat; stir in rosemary and red pepper and cool slightly.

3. Put beans, the 1½ teaspoons salt, and all but 1 teaspoon of the rosemary oil in a food processor and process until smooth. Scrape puree into a serving bowl and drizzle with reserved rosemary oil. Serve with toasted baguette and, if desired, raw vegetables.

● pantry picks

● **double duty**

● real quick

● cool tools

Prep time: 10 minutes

We wanted a new spin on shrimp cocktail. We tried many dips and loved these three so much we couldn't choose one. Make one or try all three.

grilled **shrimp** cocktail
6 servings

SHRIMP

1 **pound medium shrimp with tails, peeled and deveined**

Oil or melted butter for grilling

Kosher salt

Freshly ground black pepper

½ **lime**

Tunisian Pesto (see recipe, below)

or Fresh Green Chutney (see recipe, page 16)

or Wasabi Guacamole (see recipe, page 17)

PESTO

Makes 1 cup

2 **cups packed fresh cilantro (leaves and some stems)**

1 **cup packed fresh parsley (leaves and some stems)**

¼ **cup almonds**

1 **or 2 cloves garlic**

½ **cup extra-virgin olive oil**

½ **teaspoon kosher salt**

Pinch cayenne pepper (optional)

Preheat a grill pan or outdoor grill to medium-high. Toss shrimp with just enough oil or butter to coat lightly, then season with salt and pepper to taste. If cooking on an open grill grate, thread the shrimp on skewers or place in a grill basket. Grill shrimp until they just curl and are translucent, about 1½ minutes on each side. Squeeze lime over the shrimp and serve warm or at room temperature with dip.

TUNISIAN PESTO

1. Combine the cilantro, parsley, almonds, and garlic in a food processor and pulse until coarsely chopped. Add about ⅓ cup of the oil and process until fully incorporated and smooth. Add the salt and a pinch of cayenne pepper, if desired. Serve immediately with Grilled Shrimp (see recipe, above) or freeze.

2. If using immediately, add the remaining oil and pulse until smooth. If freezing, transfer to an airtight container and pour the remaining oil on top. Freeze up to 3 months.

COOK'S NOTE When you add raw garlic to a pesto or dip, it starts out mellow. But after garlic sits for a bit, it ends up strong. If you like your pesto intense or are adding it to a cooked dish, use both cloves—but for a tempered taste add just a single clove.

fresh **green** chutney
³/₄ cup

1 1-inch piece peeled fresh ginger

3 scallions (white and green parts), cut into large pieces

1 cup fresh mint (leaves and some stems)

1 cup fresh cilantro (leaves and some stems)

¼ cup plain yogurt

1 jalapeño, stemmed (ribs and seeds removed if you don't want dip too hot)

1 tablespoon freshly squeezed lime juice

½ teaspoon kosher salt

1 to 2 tablespoons water (optional)

With the machine running, drop ginger into the bowl of a food processor and process until coarsely chopped. Scrape down the sides of the bowl, then add scallions, mint, cilantro, yogurt, jalapeño, lime juice, and salt. Process to a textured paste similar in consistency to pesto, adding water to adjust the consistency, if desired. Serve with Grilled Shrimp (see recipe, page 14).

COOK'S NOTE This chutney is also great with grilled lamb and chicken, and super as a spread for sandwiches, rice crackers, or crispy Indian pappadum.

Speed-strip bunches of leafy herbs such as cilantro and parsley by holding them inverted at their stem end. Using a downward motion and a very sharp chef's knife, shave off the leafy greens in short, quick strokes.

wasabi guacamole
1¼ cups

| slightly heaping tablespoon wasabi powder
| tablespoon water
| ripe Hass avocado
| scallion (white and green parts), finely chopped
| tablespoon freshly squeezed lime juice
| teaspoon finely grated peeled fresh ginger
½ teaspoon mirin (a sweet Japanese rice wine) (optional)
½ teaspoon kosher salt
2 tablespoons chopped fresh cilantro

Whisk wasabi and water in a small bowl to make a thick paste; turn bowl over and set aside. Halve the avocado; press a knife into the pit, then twist and lift it out. Score the flesh with the tip of a knife, then use a spoon to scoop flesh out of skins into a medium serving bowl. Mix in the wasabi, scallion, lime juice, ginger, mirin (if desired), and salt with a fork to make a textured dip. Stir in the cilantro. Serve with Grilled Shrimp (see recipe, page 14).

COOK'S NOTE Turning the wasabi bowl upside down accomplishes two goals: The wasabi won't be quite as harsh as when it is first mixed, and its flavor will concentrate and bloom (in a good way!). This dip is great for sliced cucumbers, snow peas, or rice crackers.

● **pantry picks**

● double duty

● real quick

● cool tools

Prep time: 35 minutes

These glossy
wings are a
surefire party hit.
Just remember to
keep a stash of
napkins on hand.

blasted **balsamic chicken** wings 4 to 6 servings

½ cup red currant jelly

⅓ cup balsamic vinegar

1 teaspoon soy sauce

2 teaspoons kosher salt, plus additional for seasoning

1 teaspoon cayenne pepper

1 teaspoon garlic powder

1 teaspoon onion powder

3 pounds chicken wings (no wing tips)

1. Preheat the oven to 450°F. Line a baking sheet with aluminum foil.

2. Bring the currant jelly, vinegar, and soy sauce to a boil in a small saucepan over medium-high heat and simmer until thick and glossy, 5 to 7 minutes. While the mixture cooks, stir together the 2 teaspoons salt, cayenne, and garlic and onion powders to break up any lumps. Whisk the spices into the jelly mixture. Toss the wings with the jelly mixture in a large bowl, making sure all of the wings are coated evenly.

3. Place the chicken meaty side down on the baking sheet and reserve the excess sauce. Roast the chicken, turning halfway through cooking, until dark or almost lacquered looking, 17 to 18 minutes for small wings and up to 25 minutes for bigger, meatier wings. Then turn on the broiler and broil the chicken for 3 to 4 minutes, until wings are richly colored and glossy.

4. Toward the end of cooking the chicken, return sauce to small saucepan and bring to a boil, reduce the heat, and simmer for 1 to 2 minutes. When the wings are done, sprinkle them with salt to taste, pour the hot sauce over, toss, and serve immediately.

SHOPSMART Grocery store balsamic vinegar is an everyday condiment—it's inexpensive and great in salad dressings and sauces. The expensive stuff that comes in small bottles and vials is worth having too. Use it sparingly, drizzled over Parmesan cheese or savored with strawberries.

18

goat cheese nut log with chile

6 servings

2 tablespoons extra-virgin olive oil

Pinch crushed red pepper

¹/₂ cup toasted hazelnuts, with skin

2 teaspoons herbes de Provence

1 teaspoon finely grated lemon zest

Pinch kosher salt

Freshly ground black pepper

1 large log fresh goat cheese (about 11 ounces)

Wheat crackers or crusty bread, and sliced apples or pears for serving

1. To make the Chile Oil: Put the olive oil and red pepper in a small microwave-safe bowl and microwave on HIGH until fragrant, about 1 minute. Cool to room temperature.

2. Meanwhile, put the toasted hazelnuts, herbes de Provence, lemon zest, salt, and pepper in a minichopper and pulse until the nuts are finely ground but not pasty. Spread the nut mixture on a large plate. Roll the goat cheese in the mixture, pressing firmly to coat the whole log generously.

3. Slice the cheese into rounds and arrange on a platter. Drizzle some of the Chile Oil over the slices and serve with crackers or bread and fruit.

Gussy up plain greens with a slice of hazelnut-rolled goat cheese. Add some sliced apples or pears and you have a salad worthy of any big-city bistro.

KNOW-HOW Find a good use for all of that unflavored dental floss taking up space in your medicine cabinet—use it like we do to cut perfect rounds of goat cheese.

SAY CHEESE We are in awe of gorgeous cheese. A crumbly blue, a grating Parm, a chunky cheddar, and a runny Camembert are all you need for a well-rounded sampling.

Cheese is the original quick-and-easy.
It's great as last-minute finger food or as a light meal with bread and wine. Follow our 5 cheese tips and make the most of this simplest of starters:

SERVE cheese at room temperature (20 minutes on your counter is fine).

GO with the odds for eye appeal—three, five, or even just one cheese on a plate works.

MIX IT UP with different
• textures—soft, firm, hard
• milks—cow, goat, sheep
• places—a tour of England-France-Spain or a sampling from Vermont

PRESENT IT WITH PANACHE:
• **Do nothing.** Keep the cheese whole and let people slice their own.

• **Chunk it.** Serve hard cheese such as pecorino Romano or Parmesan in craggy nuggets.
• **Spoon it.** Lop off the top of a ripe Brie or Camembert and let guests scoop their own.

PAIR CHEESE WITH WHAT YOU HAVE:
• herb-cured olives
• marinated or pickled mushrooms or peppers
• salami, country ham, or prosciutto
• roasted nuts
• fruit chutneys
• dried apricots or figs
• fresh apples, grapes, or pears
• honey
• crusty bread

fig & almond tart

one 8-inch tart

34   saltine crackers

4   tablespoons unsalted butter, melted

1   large egg white

1/2   cup whole unblanched almonds

7   ounces dried figs (about 15), preferably Calmyrna

3/4   cup water

Freshly ground black pepper

2   tablespoons red currant jelly

1   tablespoon water

GAME PLAN: Don't bother rinsing your food processor between making the crust and the filling. Prepare the filling while the crust bakes and the almonds toast.

1. Preheat the oven to 400°F. Pulse the crackers in a food processor until finely ground; add the butter and egg white and pulse just to combine. (The mixture will look like wet, coarse sand.) Press the cracker mixture firmly with your fingers into an 8-inch cake, springform, or tart pan to make a flat crust without a raised edge. Bake until brown and dry to the touch, about 15 minutes. Spread the almonds on a small baking sheet and bake until toasted, about 10 minutes. Set the crust and almonds aside to cool.

2. Meanwhile, put figs, the 3/4 cup water, and pepper to taste in a medium saucepan; bring to a boil over high heat. Reduce heat to medium and simmer, uncovered, until figs absorb all of the water, about 10 minutes. Transfer figs to a food processor and pulse to make thick paste.

3. Put currant jelly and 1 tablespoon water in a small microwave-safe bowl and microwave on HIGH until hot and liquid, 30 to 45 seconds. Stir and set aside. Run a thin knife blade around edge of the crust and turn it out of the pan, then turn upright. Spread the fig paste over the crust, press the almonds on top, and brush lightly with the currant glaze. Cut the tart in wedges or squares and serve.

Serve this fig tart with some Cabrales blue cheese and port, and let your senses transport you to a *taberna* in the Spanish countryside.

COOK'S NOTE Use leftover figs sliced in panini (see page 55) or tossed in a salad.

Prep time: 30 minutes

pork satay
4 servings

1/3 cup water

1/3 cup freshly squeezed lime juice
     (2 to 3 limes)

3   tablespoons sugar

2   tablespoons fish sauce

1   teaspoon sambal oelek (sweet-
     hot Southeast Asian chile
     paste)

1   clove garlic, minced

1   pork tenderloin (about 1 pound)

2   tablespoons vegetable oil, plus
     additional for brushing

     Kosher salt

     Freshly ground black pepper

1   small whole carrot, finely grated

     **Boston or Bibb lettuce and
     coarsely chopped fresh mint
     and cilantro, for serving**

1. Whisk water, lime juice, sugar, and fish sauce in a small bowl until sugar dissolves. Stir in sambal oelek and garlic.

2. Slice pork crosswise into 1/2-inch-thick slices. Toss slices with about 1/4 cup of the marinade and the 2 tablespoons vegetable oil. Set aside for 15 minutes. Reserve the rest of the marinade to use as a dipping sauce.

3. Heat a grill pan or outdoor grill to medium-high heat. If you're using bamboo skewers on an outdoor grill, soak the skewers in water for 30 minutes before using. Thread one piece of pork on each skewer and lay skewers on a baking sheet or large plate. Brush the meat lightly with some oil and season with salt and pepper to taste. Working in batches, grill the skewers, without moving them, until browned on the first side, about 1 minute. Turn the skewers and grill until the second side is browned and the meat is opaque at the edges, about 1 minute more. Transfer the satays to a clean platter.

4. Stir a heaping tablespoon of grated carrot into reserved marinade to make dipping sauce. Serve satays with the sauce, remaining grated carrot, lettuce leaves, mint, and cilantro. Have guests slip pork from the skewer and wrap each piece in a lettuce leaf with some mint and cilantro.

STYLE Served on a pretty platter alongside ruffled lettuce and strewn sprigs of mint and cilantro, pork satay is an easy way to bring a touch of exotica to the table. It's also a fun icebreaker that encourages everyone to get involved at the table.

24

Prep time: 30 minutes

This stylish
Spanish tortilla—
more omelet than
bread—is the
ideal opener to a
memorable meal.

artichoke, **potato & chorizo** tortilla 6 to 8 servings

3 ounces Spanish-style chorizo,
casing removed, quartered
lengthwise, and cut into
1/4-inch-thick slices

1 medium russet potato, diced

12 ounces marinated artichoke
hearts, rinsed and drained

1 1/4 teaspoons kosher salt

1/2 teaspoon dried oregano

8 large eggs

Freshly ground black pepper

1 cup shaved or shredded
manchego, Mahon, or other
Spanish cheese (about
3 ounces)

1/4 cup jarred, sliced, roasted red
pepper, preferably piquillo
(wood-smoked peppers from
Spain)

GAME PLAN: Whisk together the eggs, salt, and pepper
while the potatoes brown with the chorizo and artichokes.

1. Position a rack about 6 inches from the broiler and
preheat. Set a medium ovenproof nonstick skillet over
medium-high heat. Add the chorizo, potato, artichokes,
1/4 teaspoon salt, and the oregano and cook, stirring
occasionally, until the potato is brown and tender, about
10 minutes. Meanwhile, whisk the eggs with the remaining
1 teaspoon salt and black pepper to taste.

2. Pull the skillet from the heat, pour the eggs over the
vegetables, and stir just until they begin to set. Scatter the
cheese over the eggs and top with the red pepper. Broil
the tortilla until the eggs are set, about 2 minutes. Use a
rubber spatula or wooden spoon to loosen the eggs from
the side of the skillet and slide the tortilla onto a cutting
board. Slice into thin wedges and serve.

STYLE Serve the tortilla either straight from the pan or at
room temperature with a glass of sherry and a dish of
almonds.

fresh cheese quesadillas with
arugula & radish 4 servings

To start the meal or be the meal, our mod riff on quesadillas brings fresh and rich flavors into the fold.

QUESADILLAS

- **4**   8-inch flour tortillas
- **⅓**   cup soft cheese, such as fresh goat, ricotta, or crumbled feta
- **½**   medium bunch arugula
- **3**   radishes, sliced
-      Kosher salt

SALSA

- **1**   pound vine-ripe tomatoes (about 2 tomatoes)
- **¼**   small red onion
- **1**   tablespoon chopped fresh cilantro
- **1**   teaspoon chipotle hot sauce
- **1**   teaspoon kosher salt

GAME PLAN: Make the Quick Tomato Salsa before cooking the quesadillas. Have all of your ingredients for the quesadillas prepped and ready next to the burner.

To make the quesadillas: Toast a tortilla directly over a gas burner (or in a dry cast-iron skillet if you have electric burners), turning it with tongs occasionally until slightly blistered on both sides. Transfer the tortilla to a work surface. Scatter some cheese on half the tortilla and top with some arugula leaves and radish slices. Season with salt to taste. Fold the tortilla over and press firmly. Repeat with the remaining ingredients. Serve warm or at room temperature with the salsa.

QUICK TOMATO SALSA

Halve the tomatoes and grate them on the largest side of a box grater into a bowl, discarding the skins. Grate the onion into the tomato and then stir in the cilantro, hot sauce, and salt.

KNOW-HOW Grating tomatoes and onions on the large-hole side of a box grater is a speedy alternative to chopping.

thai shrimp & rice soup • slow-cooker bean & barley soup • black bean soup with mojo • chicken, spinach & gnocchi soup • tortilla soup • gazpacho • mushroom miso soup • celery, tuna & white bean salad • summer tomato bread salad with scallops • bistro bacon & egg salad • romesco salad • roast beef salad with pears, blue cheese & nuts • grilled chicken salad with honey-ginger dressing • crustless spinach & feta pies • salami & provolone panini • monte cristos • antipasta pizza

soups, salads & sandwiches

Our fresh takes on fast and casual meals hit the spot any time.

thai **shrimp & rice** soup

4 servings

4 cups chicken broth, low-sodium
   canned

1 to 2 teaspoons chile-garlic
   sauce (also called sri racha)

1 rib celery, thinly sliced on an
   angle

1 medium carrot, peeled,
   quartered lengthwise, and
   thinly sliced

1 4-inch piece lemongrass, thinly
   sliced (see how-to, below)

2 tablespoons fish sauce

2 teaspoons sugar

1 pound medium shrimp without
   tails, peeled and deveined

2 cups cooked rice, preferably
   jasmine

   Freshly squeezed juice of
   1 lemon (3 to 4 tablespoons)

½ cup coarsely chopped fresh
   cilantro (leaves only)

GAME PLAN: Chop the lemongrass and cilantro while the broth simmers.

1. Put the chicken broth, chile-garlic sauce, celery, and carrot in a medium saucepan and bring to a simmer. Add the lemongrass, fish sauce, and sugar and simmer another 5 minutes.

2. Stir in the shrimp and rice and simmer just until the shrimp are pink and opaque, 2 to 3 minutes more.

3. Pull the saucepan from the heat and stir in the lemon juice and cilantro. Ladle the soup into warmed bowls.

SHOPSMART Keep prepeeled and deveined shrimp on hand in the freezer. They defrost quickly in a bowl with running water flowing over it.

Twice is nice when it comes to rice, so next time make a double batch. Use the leftovers in this soup, a salad, or stuffing.

1. Remove the tough outer layers of the lemongrass stalk (usually two or three pieces). **2.** Cut off the root end of the lemongrass. **3.** Place your knife flat against the root end and trim stalk. **4.** Slice the stalk starting at the bottom and moving up until it becomes too tough and woody.

pantry picks

double duty

real quick

cool tools

Prep time: 10 minutes active time (8 hours in slow cooker)
Special equipment: slow cooker

Slow cookers rock! Load yours up in the morning and you're rewarded with a hearty home-cooked meal at the end of the day.

slow-cooker bean & barley soup 4 to 6 servings

1 cup dried multibean mix or Great Northern beans, picked over and rinsed

6 cups water

1 14-ounce can whole tomatoes, with juice

3 cloves garlic, smashed

2 ribs celery, chopped

2 medium carrots, chopped

½ medium onion, chopped

½ cup pearl barley

1 bay leaf

1½ tablespoons kosher salt, plus additional for seasoning

2 teaspoons dried Italian herb blend

Freshly ground black pepper

½ ounce dried porcini mushrooms (optional)

3 cups cleaned baby spinach leaves (about 3 ounces)

1 cup freshly grated Parmesan cheese

1 tablespoon balsamic vinegar

Extra-virgin olive oil

1. Put beans, water, tomatoes and their juices, garlic, celery, carrots, onion, barley, bay leaf, 1½ tablespoons salt, herb blend, pepper, and porcini mushrooms (if desired) in a slow cooker; cover and cook on LOW until the beans are quite tender and the soup is thick, about 8 hours.

2. Stir in the spinach, cheese, and vinegar, cover, and let the soup be until the spinach wilts, about 5 minutes. Remove and discard bay leaf. Taste and season with salt and black pepper to taste.

3. Ladle the soup into warmed bowls and drizzle each serving with olive oil.

KNOW-HOW We like to stir in spinach just at the end of cooking and drizzle in extra-virgin olive oil right before serving. The warm soup gently wilts the greens and coaxes out nuances in the olive oil that add a whole new dimension of flavor.

Prep time: 20 minutes active time (8 hours in slow cooker)
Special equipment: slow cooker

black bean **soup with** mojo
8 to 10 servings

Garlicky Cuban mojo sauce can work its magic on anything. Besides bolstering our black bean soup, it gives jarred salsa a jolt and perks up grilled pork chops.

SOUP

2 cups (I pound) dried black beans, picked over and rinsed

4 country-style blade pork ribs (about 2 pounds)

8 cups water

¼ cup dark rum

I head garlic, unpeeled, halved horizontally to expose the cloves

I medium onion, chopped

2 tablespoons kosher salt

2 bay leaves

I teaspoon dried oregano

I teaspoon ground cumin

I teaspoon crushed red pepper

MOJO

4 cloves garlic, chopped

¼ cup extra-virgin olive oil

½ cup freshly squeezed lime juice (about 4 limes)

¼ cup chopped fresh cilantro

I teaspoon kosher salt

I. Put black beans, pork ribs, water, rum, garlic head halves, onion, salt, bay leaves, oregano, cumin, and crushed red pepper in a slow cooker; cover and cook on LOW until the beans are tender and the meat is falling off the rib bones, about 8 hours.

2. Remove the ribs from the soup. Using a handheld (immersion) blender, partially puree the soup until it is creamy but still has some texture from whole beans. (Or puree half the soup in a blender and stir it back into the slow cooker.) Pull the meat from the rib bones, shredding it into large pieces, and stir it into the soup.

3. Ladle the soup into warmed bowls and drizzle each serving with some mojo. Pass the remaining mojo.

MOJO

Put the garlic and olive oil in a small microwave-safe bowl and microwave on HIGH until the garlic is golden, I to 2 minutes. Stir in the lime juice, cilantro, and salt and set aside until ready to serve.

SHOPSMART Country-style pork ribs are a smart buy—they're meatier and plumper than spareribs but just as economical.

33

pantry picks

double duty

real quick

cool tools

chicken, **spinach & gnocchi soup** 4 servings

Kosher salt

2 cups prepared gnocchi

4 cups chicken broth, low-sodium canned

4 cloves garlic, thinly sliced

2 tablespoons unsalted butter

Pinch sugar

3 cups cleaned baby spinach leaves

2 cups shredded cooked chicken

Freshly ground black pepper

Hunk of good Parmesan or other grana-style (hard grating) cheese

1. Bring a medium saucepan of cold water to a boil over high heat, then salt it generously. Add the gnocchi and cook, stirring occasionally, until al dente, about 3 minutes. Drain and set aside.

2. Meanwhile, put ¼ cup of the chicken broth, garlic, butter, and sugar in a large saucepan over medium-low heat, bring it to a simmer, and cook, uncovered, until the garlic is tender, about 1 minute. Add the spinach and let it wilt for about 30 seconds. Add the remaining 3¾ cups chicken broth and the chicken and bring just to a simmer. Stir in the gnocchi and bring to a full boil. Taste and season with salt and a generous amount of pepper to taste—use a light hand with the salt because the cheese is salty.

3. Ladle the soup into warmed shallow bowls and shower each with some freshly grated cheese.

Hey, your market isn't called "super" for nothing. Take a quick spin through and grab a rotisserie chicken and these ready-to-go ingredients. They'll help you get your soup on in a flash.

COOK'S NOTE Save your leftover rinds of Parmesan and add to soups, braises, and sauces. It beefs up flavor and also makes use of every ounce of your pricey Parmesan.

Add a swirl of chile and homey tortillas to comforting chicken soup and you have a bold hug of a meal.

tortilla soup

4 servings

2 tablespoons vegetable oil

1 medium onion, chopped

2 cloves garlic, sliced

1 chipotle chile *en adobo*, minced

1 tablespoon chili powder

2 teaspoons kosher salt

6 cups chicken broth, low-sodium canned

1 cup corn kernels, fresh or frozen and thawed

1 ripe tomato, chopped

1 cup shredded cooked chicken

½ cup cilantro leaves

¼ cup freshly squeezed lime juice (about 2 limes)

About a dozen corn tortilla chips, broken a bit

Lime wedges (optional)

1. Heat the oil in a medium saucepan over medium heat. Add the onion, garlic, chipotle, chili powder, and salt and cook until the onion softens, about 5 minutes. Add the chicken broth, bring to a boil, reduce the heat slightly, and simmer, uncovered, for 10 minutes. Add the corn and cook for 5 minutes more.

2. Pull the saucepan from the heat and stir in the tomato, chicken, cilantro, and lime juice. Divide the tortilla chips among 4 warmed bowls, ladle the soup on top, and serve with lime wedges, if desired.

KNOW-HOW Get every last drop of juice from those little limes. Before halving, microwave them for a few seconds and roll them under the palm of your hand to release the juice from the pulp.

gazpacho
4 servings

Classic and cool,
fresh and fast
never go out
of style.

2 cloves garlic

1 tablespoon kosher salt, plus additional for seasoning

2 pounds ripe tomatoes, cored and quartered

2 Kirby cucumbers (or ½ of a peeled regular cucumber or 4 inches of an English cucumber) (about ½ pound), quartered and cut into 2-inch pieces

3 scallions (white and green parts), quartered

1 small poblano pepper, seeded and roughly chopped

2 cups chilled tomato juice

2 to 3 tablespoons sherry or red wine vinegar

¼ teaspoon hot sauce

2 or 3 ice cubes

¼ cup extra-virgin olive oil, plus additional for garnish

⅓ cup fresh flat-leaf parsley

⅓ cup fresh mint

Freshly ground black pepper

1. Smash the garlic cloves, sprinkle with the 1 tablespoon salt, and, with the flat side of a large knife, mash and smear the mixture to a coarse paste. Put the paste in a large bowl and toss with the tomatoes, cucumbers, scallions, poblano, tomato juice, vinegar, hot sauce, and ice.

2. Working in batches, ladle the mixture into a blender and process to make a slightly coarse puree, then transfer to a serving bowl. With the last batch, while the motor is running, drizzle in the ¼ cup olive oil until incorporated. Chop the parsley and mint by hand or in a minichopper and stir most of the herbs into the soup. Season the soup with salt and black pepper to taste.

3. Ladle the soup into chilled bowls, scatter the reserved herbs over the soup, and drizzle with olive oil.

SHOPSMART Why buy regular cukes when you can buy Kirbys? Also called pickling cucumbers, small 3- to 6-inch-long Kirby cucumbers are always unwaxed, which is why they're a time-saver—they never need to be peeled.

● pantry picks

● double duty

● **real quick**

● cool tools

Prep time: 15 minutes

mushroom **miso** soup

4 servings

4 cups boxed shiitake mushroom-flavored Japanese-style soup broth

4 shiitake mushrooms, stems removed, caps thinly sliced

1 cup baby spinach leaves or large leaves, torn

¼ cup grated carrot

3 tablespoons shiro miso (white fermented soybean paste)

8 ounces soft tofu, blotted dry and cut into ½-inch cubes

¼ cup thinly sliced scallions (green part only)

GAME PLAN: Grate the carrot, cube the tofu, and slice the scallions while the broth simmers.

Put the broth and sliced shiitake mushrooms in a medium saucepan and simmer until the mushrooms are soft, about 3 minutes. Add the spinach and carrot and cook until the spinach wilts, about 1 minute. Remove from the heat, whisk in the miso until smooth, and add the tofu and scallions. Ladle the soup into warmed bowls and serve.

KNOW-HOW If reheating this soup, don't let it boil. The intense heat changes the flavor of the miso.

celery, **tuna &** white bean
salad 4 servings

Hold the mayo! For tuna salad with attitude, jazz it up instead with bold Mediterranean flavors.

SALAD

- 4 ribs celery, thinly sliced on an angle
- 1 15-ounce can white beans, drained and rinsed
- ½ cup pickled button mushrooms, with a little bit of their liquid
- ¼ cup chopped pitted kalamata olives
- 1 tablespoon capers, drained
- 1 rounded tablespoon whole-grain mustard

  Freshly squeezed juice from a good-size lemon wedge
- 1 teaspoon kosher salt

  Freshly ground black pepper
- 1 12-ounce can oil-packed tuna
- 1 cup ripe cherry or grape tomatoes, halved
- 5 cups mixed greens

  Grilled or toasted pocketless pita bread

  Lemon wedges (optional)

PITA BREAD

- 2 6-inch pocketless pita rounds

  Extra-virgin olive oil

  Kosher salt

1. Toss the celery with the beans, mushrooms and liquid, olives, capers, mustard, lemon juice, salt, and pepper to taste. Drain the tuna. Add the tuna and tomatoes; toss to break up the tuna and coat the salad with the dressing.

2. Spread the greens on a serving platter and spoon the salad on top. Arrange the pita and lemon wedges (if desired) around the greens and serve.

GRILLED POCKETLESS PITA BREAD

Preheat a grill pan over medium heat. Lightly brush both sides of the bread with olive oil and season with salt to taste. Grill until golden, turning once, about 4 minutes. Cut into wedges and serve warm. (The pita may be grilled on an outdoor gas or charcoal grill too.)

SHOPSMART Oil-packed tuna is more flavorful and has a nicer consistency than its water-packed cousin.

In high summer, when the sun is strong and the tomatoes are ripe, make panzanella. An especially fine use for day-old bread, this meal begs to be eaten alfresco.

summer tomato bread salad with scallops 4 servings

1½	pounds ripe tomatoes
1	shallot, minced
4	cloves garlic, minced
⅓	cup extra-virgin olive oil, plus additional for grilling
2	tablespoons red wine vinegar
1	slightly heaping tablespoon kosher salt, plus additional to taste
	Freshly ground black pepper
10	ounces stale country-style bread, torn into large pieces
1	cup fresh basil leaves
12	medium sea scallops (about 12 ounces)

1. Core the tomatoes and, if large, cut them into chunks; if small, halve or quarter them. Toss them gently with the shallot, garlic, oil, vinegar, 1 tablespoon salt, and pepper. Set aside until the tomatoes are very juicy, about 10 minutes.

2. Meanwhile, preheat a grill pan or heat an outdoor grill to medium heat. Fill a large bowl with ice water. Add the bread and set aside until soft, no more than 5 minutes. Using your hands, scoop the bread from the water, squeeze out as much water as possible, and rub it through your fingers into the tomatoes. Tear the basil over the salad and toss gently. (The bread salad can be served now or set aside at room temperature for a couple of hours.)

3. Lightly brush the scallops with olive oil and season with salt and pepper to taste. Grill the scallops, turning once, until firm but not tough, about 2 minutes per side. Cut the scallops in half, add to the bread salad, and serve.

COOK'S NOTE It's easy to dry fresh bread. Tear it into chunks and microwave for 1 to 2 minutes. Or place the chunked bread on a baking sheet in a 250°F oven for a few minutes. Done.

● pantry picks

● double duty

● **real quick**

● cool tools

Prep time: 15 minutes

Rustic and elegant, our bistro salad climbs to heights that bacon and eggs never could reach alone.

bistro **bacon & egg** salad

4 servings

4 slices bacon, cut crosswise into thin strips

2½ tablespoons cider vinegar

2 teaspoons Dijon mustard

Kosher salt

Freshly ground black pepper

2 tablespoons extra-virgin olive oil

8 large eggs

8 cups mesclun salad greens (about 7 ounces)

4 to 8 slices crusty bread, toasted if desired

I. Cook the bacon in a medium skillet over medium heat, stirring occasionally, until crisp. Using a slotted spoon, transfer the bacon to a paper towel. Pull the skillet from the heat (leave drippings in the skillet) and stir in 1½ tablespoons cider vinegar, scraping up any browned bits clinging to the skillet. Pour the mixture into a large bowl and whisk in mustard, salt and pepper to taste, and olive oil.

2. Fill a nonstick skillet with about 2 inches of water and bring it to the barest simmer over medium heat; add the remaining I tablespoon vinegar. Crack the eggs, slipping them gently into the water, and cook until the whites are set but the yolks are still runny, about 4 minutes.

3. While the eggs poach, toss the greens with the vinaigrette and bits of bacon. Divide the salad among 4 plates or shallow bowls. Using a slotted spoon, gently scoop the eggs from the water, blot dry with a paper towel, and place 2 of them on top of each salad. Add bread to each plate and serve.

STYLE Our bistro salad cries out for a glass of crisp, fruity rosé.

romesco **salad**

4 servings

8 whole scallions, trimmed

⅓ cup extra-virgin olive oil

Kosher salt

Freshly ground black pepper

3 slices country-style bread
(about ½ inch thick)

1 clove garlic

8 roasted red peppers, preferably
piquillo (wood-smoked peppers
from Spain), roughly chopped

½ cup pitted green olives, roughly
chopped

¼ heaping cup whole almonds,
toasted and chopped

1 tablespoon sherry vinegar

1½ teaspoons pimenton (Spanish-
style smoked paprika), plus
additional for seasoning

½ head romaine lettuce, torn into
pieces

Chunk of Manchego cheese
(about 5 ounces)

2 ounces very thinly sliced
Serrano ham or prosciutto
(optional)

1. Heat a large grill pan over high heat. Lightly brush the scallions with some olive oil and season with salt and pepper to taste. Grill the scallions, turning occasionally, until charred and soft, about 4 minutes. Lightly brush the bread with oil and grill on both sides until toasted. Rub the toast with the garlic clove.

2. Chop the scallions into 1-inch pieces and put them in a large bowl with the roasted red peppers, olives, almonds, vinegar, and paprika and toss to combine. Add the romaine, drizzle with the remaining olive oil (about ¼ cup), season with salt and pepper, and toss. Tear the bread into small pieces and toss into the salad.

3. Divide the salad among 4 plates and, using a vegetable peeler, cut large shavings of cheese over each. Drape some ham over each salad (if desired), sprinkle with paprika, and serve.

We're crazy about romesco sauce, a Catalonian condiment, but when pressed for time, we toss all the essential elements in a salad topped with cheese and ham. We're in heaven!

roast beef salad with pears,
blue cheese & nuts 6 servings

SALAD

8   cups mesclun salad greens (about 7 ounces)

2   endives, thinly sliced crosswise

2   ripe pears, preferably red Bartlett, Comice, or Forelle

10 ounces rare roast beef, thinly sliced

3   ounces blue cheese, such as Roquefort, Maytag, or Stilton

¼   cup toasted hazelnuts, skins removed (rub them in a clean cotton towel while still warm)

    Kosher salt

    Freshly ground black pepper

    Honey-Mustard and Hazelnut Vinaigrette (see recipe, below)

VINAIGRETTE
Makes I cup

2   tablespoons honey-Dijon mustard

2   tablespoons apple cider vinegar

I   teaspoon kosher salt

    Freshly ground black pepper

I   cup hazelnut oil or a mixture of half hazelnut, half extra-virgin olive oil

Toss the mesclun with the endives in a large bowl. Halve and core the pears and slice them very thin lengthwise—use a mandoline if you have one. Add the pear slices to the greens along with the roast beef, blue cheese, and hazelnuts. Season the salad with salt and pepper to taste and toss with all of the dressing. Divide the salad among 4 chilled plates and serve.

HONEY-MUSTARD AND HAZELNUT VINAIGRETTE

Whisk the mustard, vinegar, salt, and pepper to taste in a small bowl. Gradually whisk in the oil, starting with a few drops and then adding the rest in a steady stream, to make a smooth, slightly thick dressing.

COOK'S NOTE Nut oils can be pricey, but the fast hit of deep flavor they bring to steamed vegetables, marinades, and cold sauces is worth every penny. Store them in your fridge to extend their life up to 3 months.

Salads from grab-and-go items are terrific. Choose flavors and textures that flatter one another, and they make the ideal instant meal—tasty, surprising, and so, so easy.

● pantry picks

● studio dozy

● real quick

● cool tools

Prep time: 15 minutes

Indoor grill pans rule. Though cooked inside, food looks as if it's been kissed by charcoal—a definite winter pick-me-up.

grilled chicken salad with honey-ginger dressing
4 servings

4 boneless, skinless chicken breasts (1½ to 2 pounds)

5 tablespoons extra-virgin olive oil

 Kosher salt

 Freshly ground black pepper

1 tablespoon freshly squeezed lemon juice

1 tablespoon honey

1 teaspoon grated peeled fresh ginger

8 cups mesclun salad greens (about 7 ounces)

1 ripe mango, peeled and cut into bite-size chunks (see how-to, below)

GAME PLAN: While the chicken is grilling, cut the mango and make the vinaigrette.

1. For the chicken: Heat a grill pan over medium-high heat. Brush the chicken with 1 tablespoon of the olive oil, then season with salt and pepper to taste. Place the chicken smooth side down on the grill and cook until the edges turn opaque, about 6 minutes. (To get crosshatch grill marks, about halfway through cooking rotate breasts about 45 degrees.) Turn the chicken over and cook until firm to the touch, about 6 minutes more. Transfer the chicken to a cutting board and let rest for 5 minutes.

2. For the dressing: Meanwhile, combine the lemon juice, honey, and ginger in a small bowl. Gradually whisk in the remaining ¼ cup olive oil, starting with a few drops and then adding the rest in a steady stream, to make a smooth, slightly thick dressing.

3. To assemble the salad: Slice or shred the chicken into pieces and add it to the greens along with the mango and the vinaigrette. Toss; divide the salad among 4 large plates and serve.

1. Set the mango on its side and slice ½ inch from each end. 2. Stand mango upright, look down over it, then sliver away skin from top to bottom. 3. Slice away the two fat sides by running your knife along the pit. Repeat with edges of mango. 4. Slice each half into planks, then chop each plank into cubes.

Prep time: 1 hour (including baking time)

crustless **spinach & feta** pies

4 servings

You'll be crazy about our quick take on spanakopita. Plated with a zesty tomato salad, this is an impressive dressy lunch or light dinner you can throw together with ease.

PIES

1	tablespoon extra-virgin olive oil
1	10-ounce package frozen spinach, thawed
4	scallions, thinly sliced
3	large eggs
¾	cup half-and-half
1	tablespoon plain bread crumbs
2	teaspoons crumbled dried mint
1¼	teaspoons kosher salt
	Freshly ground black pepper
	Pinch cayenne pepper
	Freshly grated nutmeg
⅓	cup crumbled feta cheese

TOMATO SALAD

12	ounces mixed small tomatoes
2	to 3 pepperoncini, stemmed and chopped
2	tablespoons pitted kalamata olives, coarsely chopped
2	tablespoons olive oil
1	tablespoon freshly squeezed lemon juice
¼	teaspoon dried oregano
	Kosher salt
	Freshly ground black pepper

1. Position a rack in the center of the oven and preheat to 400°F. Heat olive oil in a medium skillet over medium-high heat. Squeeze excess water out of spinach. Add spinach and scallions and cook, stirring, until dry, about 4 minutes. Transfer to a colander and press with the back of a spoon to remove the last bit of moisture. Brush four 6-ounce ramekins with some olive oil and put on a baking sheet.

2. Put spinach mixture, eggs, half-and-half, bread crumbs, mint, salt, black and cayenne peppers, and nutmeg in a food processor and pulse until spinach is finely chopped. Remove blade and stir in feta cheese. Divide mixture evenly among ramekins. Bake until set around the edges but still slightly soft in the center, about 20 minutes. Turn oven off, leaving pies inside to set, about 5 minutes more.

3. Run a knife around edge of each pie and invert onto plates; spoon some tomato salad around each and serve.

GREEK TOMATO SALAD

Toss tomatoes with pepperoncini and olives in a salad bowl. Add olive oil, lemon juice, oregano, and salt and black pepper to taste. Toss again.

SHOPSMART Deep into summer, we stock up on heirloom tomatoes. Grown from the prized seeds of nearly forgotten varieties, these sweet, succulent beauties are a treat in a salad or simply sliced and sprinkled with salt.

● pantry picks
● double-duty
● real quick
● cool tools

Prep time: 20 minutes

Who says a
sandwich can't be
cool? Versatile,
fast, and outfitted
with any style of
filling, panini
deserve their
superstar status.

salami & provolone panini
4 servings

8 slices (about ⅜ inch thick)
country-style white bread

½ cup prepared onion jam

6 ounces sliced provolone cheese

4 ounces sliced hard salami, such
as soppressata or cappicola

4 teaspoons Dijon mustard

I clove garlic, halved

Extra-virgin olive oil, for
brushing the pan

I. Heat a sandwich press or a grill pan over medium heat. (If you don't have either one, use a cast-iron or heavy-bottomed skillet.) Spread I side of all the bread with I tablespoon onion jam. Top half the bread with a few pieces of provolone and then some salami. Spread I teaspoon mustard over the salami and top with the remaining bread, jam side down.

2. Rub both sides of each panino with the garlic clove. If using a sandwich press, cook the sandwiches, I or 2 at a time, until the bread is golden brown and the cheese has melted, about 4 minutes. If using a grill pan or skillet, brush it lightly with olive oil, add I or 2 panini, and cook, pressing with a spatula, for about I½ minutes, then turn and cook, pressing, until the bread is golden brown and the cheese has melted, about I½ minutes more. Halve and serve immediately.

SHOPSMART Great panini need strong shoulders to lean on, and crusty bread is the natural choice. If you don't use the entire loaf, slice the rest and freeze for the next time you need a quick sandwich.

Panini are the ultimate "use what you have" meal. Leftover roasted meat, cheese, fresh or dried fruit, and spreads make good fillings. Whether paired with milk or Merlot, the possibilities are infinite.

PERFECT PANINI

- Use a cast-iron or heavy-bottomed skillet if you don't have a sandwich press (waffle irons don't work!).

- Multigrain bread is a healthy alternative to white bread.
- Leftover roasted or grilled vegetables make great fillings.

LAWS TO PRESS BY:
- Limit fillings to four.
- Use dry ingredients so your panini don't get soggy.
- Forgo leafy greens and mayonnaise (neither is tempting when warm).
- Use a light hand when brushing bread with oil.

STAFF FAVORITES:
- Roast asparagus with goat cheese and olive spread
- Smoked trout with horseradish cream cheese and apple slices
- Roast turkey with jalapeño Jack cheese and cranberry relish
- Smoked ham with fontina
- Leftover roast lamb with Tunisian Pesto (see page 14)
- Nutella with orange marmalade

monte cristos
4 servings

¼ cup Dijon mustard

¼ cup mayonnaise

8 slices challah bread (about 1 inch thick)

6 ounces sliced Muenster cheese

12 ounces thinly sliced cooked turkey breast

Kosher salt

Freshly ground black pepper

⅔ cup whole-berry cranberry sauce or relish

3 large eggs

¼ cup milk

4 tablespoons unsalted butter

1. Mix the mustard and mayonnaise together in a small bowl. Lay the bread on a work surface and spread about 1 tablespoon of the mustard mixture on one side of each piece.

2. Lay the cheese on half of the bread slices, top with the turkey, and season with salt and pepper to taste. Spread the cranberry sauce on the remaining 4 bread slices and close the sandwiches, pressing each one together slightly.

3. In a pie plate or other shallow dish, whisk the eggs with the milk and salt and pepper to taste. Heat 2 large skillets over medium-low heat and divide the butter between them. Dip each sandwich in the egg mixture to coat completely—including the sides. Lay 2 sandwiches in each skillet and cook until bread is golden brown and cheese has melted, turning once, about 5 minutes per side. Halve and serve immediately.

Everyone knows Thanksgiving leftovers are tastier than the meal itself. This sandwich, which uses both cranberry sauce and roast turkey, is no exception.

COOK'S NOTE We like our Monte Cristos with other meats, too, such as leftover roast pork or chicken.

- pantry picks
- double duty
- **real quick**
- cool tools

Prep time: 25 minutes (with prepared dough)

antipasta pizza
4 to 6 servings

Homemade pizza faster than delivery? You bet! With our recipe for homemade 'za, you'll be sofa surfing—slice in hand—in less than 30 minutes.

TOPPING

- 4 medium ripe tomatoes (about 1½ pounds), diced
- 3 ounces thinly sliced cappicola, torn into bite-size pieces
- ½ cup pepperoncini, stemmed and roughly chopped (about 18)

  Kosher salt
- 2 10-ounce tubes prepared pizza dough or No-Fuss Pizza Dough (see recipe, below)

  Extra-virgin olive oil
- 6 ounces fresh goat or feta cheese
- ½ cup torn fresh basil
- 1 tablespoon chopped fresh oregano

DOUGH

- 1 cup tepid water (about 100°F)
- 3 tablespoons extra-virgin olive oil, plus additional as needed
- 2 teaspoons sugar
- 1½ teaspoons kosher salt
- 3 cups all-purpose flour, plus additional for kneading
- 1½ teaspoons active dry yeast

1. Preheat the oven to 425°F. Mix together the tomatoes, cappicola, and pepperoncini and season with salt to taste.

2. Line the backs of 2 baking sheets with parchment paper. **For prepared dough:** Unroll one tube of dough on a work surface and gently stretch into an 11x16-inch rectangle. Transfer to a prepared pan. Repeat with the other dough. **For homemade dough:** Dust work surface lightly with flour. Flatten a ball of dough. Press the edge with your fingers, rotating and stretching it into a disk about 10 inches across. Transfer to a prepared pan. Cover with a kitchen towel. Repeat to make 3 more crusts.

3. Brush a little olive oil over each crust and crumble cheese evenly on top. Scatter tomato mixture over crusts (hold back juice or crust will get soggy). Bake until bottom is brown and crust is crisp, 15 to 18 minutes. Sprinkle basil and oregano over pizza and serve.

NO-FUSS PIZZA DOUGH

Stir water, oil, sugar, and salt in a liquid measuring cup until sugar dissolves. Whisk flour and yeast in a large bowl. Make a well in the center and add liquid. With a wooden spoon or your hand, stir flour into liquid to make a rough dough. Pull dough into a ball. Turn dough onto a work surface dusted with flour. Knead until dough is smooth and elastic, about 5 minutes, using a little flour if necessary to keep from sticking. Divide dough into 4 equal portions, form into balls, and put on a lightly oiled baking sheet. Brush tops with oil, cover with plastic wrap, and set aside to rise until doubled, about 45 minutes.

sesame noodles with chicken • brothy japanese noodles with mushrooms & tofu • spaghetti with spicy greens & garlic • bowties with cauliflower, olives & lemon • weekday italian gravy • singapore fried rice • risotto with winter vegetables • shrimp & saffron risotto • beef & bulgur pilaf with mint • skillet cornbread pudding with ham & pepper jack

pasta & grains

Bowls of comfort with global meal appeal.

sesame noodles with chicken

4 to 6 servings

Kosher salt

1 pound spaghetti or Chinese egg noodles

2 tablespoons toasted sesame oil

1 garlic clove, peeled

1 1-inch piece peeled fresh ginger

½ cup smooth peanut butter

¼ cup soy sauce

2 tablespoons dark brown sugar

1 tablespoon rice vinegar

¾ teaspoon crushed red pepper

¼ cup hot water

1 kirby cucumber, halved and sliced

1 cup shredded cooked chicken

6 scallions (white and green parts), sliced

¼ cup dry-roasted peanuts, chopped

GAME PLAN: Make the sauce while the noodles cook.

1. Bring a large pot of cold water to a boil over high heat. When the pasta water boils, salt it generously, add the spaghetti or noodles, and cook, stirring occasionally, until al dente. Drain and rinse under cold running water. Put the spaghetti in a large bowl and toss with the sesame oil.

2. To make the Peanut Sauce: In a blender drop in the garlic and ginger while the motor is running. When the chopping is complete, stop the machine and add the peanut butter, soy sauce, brown sugar, vinegar, and red pepper. Process until smooth, then—with the blender running—slowly pour in the water.

3. To serve, toss the spaghetti with the Peanut Sauce, then top with the cucumber, chicken, scallions, and peanuts.

COOK'S NOTE Toasted sesame oil delivers richness and intensity to our sesame sauce with just a drizzle. Maintain its punch by storing it in your fridge.

pantry picks

double duty

real quick

cool tools

Prep time: 30 minutes

White-hot and
super cool, tofu is
one of the most
versatile players
to have on hand.
Teamed up with
just about any
sauce or spice,
it's one of
our favorite
building blocks.

brothy japanese noodles with mushrooms & tofu

4 servings

⅓ cup soy sauce

3 tablespoons rice vinegar

2 tablespoons mirin (sweet Japanese rice wine)

2 tablespoons peanut oil

1 tablespoon toasted sesame oil

1 2-inch piece peeled fresh ginger, finely grated

2 blocks firm tofu (about 24 ounces), blotted dry

1 pound portobello mushroom caps (about 6 medium)

2 tablespoons *gomashio* (see tip, below), plus additional for garnish

Kosher salt

2 small bundles soba noodles (about 11 ounces)

4 scallions (white and green parts), thinly sliced

1 teaspoon chile oil

SHOPSMART Japanese soba (buckwheat noodles) can be found in most supermarkets' ethnic or organic food aisle, which is where you'll also find *gomashio*, a sesame seed spice blend that supplies big effects with little effort. You can substitute toasted sesame seeds in a pinch.

1. Position an oven rack about 6 inches from the broiler and preheat. Line a large broiler pan with aluminum foil. Whisk the soy sauce with the vinegar, mirin, peanut oil, sesame oil, and ginger in a large bowl.

2. Stand the tofu blocks on end and halve top to bottom, then halve the slices to make 8 pieces. (If you like your tofu crispy, cut it into smaller pieces.) Arrange the tofu and mushroom caps on the broiler pan, pour about half the soy sauce mixture over, and turn the tofu and caps to coat thoroughly. Set aside for at least 5 or up to 30 minutes. Broil the tofu and mushrooms until the mushroom caps start to brown and shrink, about 5 minutes. Turn, sprinkle 1 tablespoon of the *gomashio* over the tofu and continue to broil until the mushrooms are soft and the tofu is glazed, about 5 minutes more.

3. Meanwhile, bring a medium saucepan of water to a boil. When the water boils, salt it generously, add the soba noodles, and cook until slightly tender, about 2 minutes. Add 1 cup of cold water to the pot, return it to a simmer, and cook the noodles until al dente, about 2 minutes more. Scoop out ¼ cup of the noodle cooking water and add it to the remaining soy mixture. Drain the noodles and add them to the soy mixture along with the scallions, chile oil, and remaining 1 tablespoon *gomashio*; toss to coat.

4. Slice the mushroom caps. Divide the noodles among 4 bowls and top them with the tofu and mushroom slices and more *gomashio*.

pantry picks

double duty

real quick

cool tools

Prep time: 25 minutes

We must keep the garlic industry afloat. We buy ropes and ropes of the stuff. There's no such thing as too much garlic.

spaghetti with spicy greens & garlic 6 servings

I½ teaspoons kosher salt, plus additional for pasta water

16 cloves peeled garlic, thinly sliced

⅓ cup extra-virgin olive oil

2 medium yellow onions, halved and sliced

⅛ teaspoon crushed red pepper

12 cups torn greens, such as mustard, kale, chard, escarole, or a mix

12 ounces spaghetti

¼ cup grated pecorino Romano cheese

KNOW-HOW Speed-wash your greens like we do here in the Food Network Kitchens: Tear up the leaves, swish them in a big bowl of water, shake them semidry, and get cooking.

GAME PLAN: Slice the garlic and onions while the water boils. Wash and tear the greens while the onions brown.

I. Bring a large pot of cold water to a boil and salt it generously. Cook garlic in olive oil in a large skillet over medium-high heat, stirring occasionally, until golden brown and crispy, about 3 minutes; take care that the garlic doesn't get too brown or it will be bitter. Using a slotted spoon, transfer the garlic chips to a paper towel. Pour off and reserve all but 2 tablespoons oil. Add the onions and red pepper (add a little more if you like things spicy) to the skillet and cook, stirring, until light brown, about 10 minutes. Season with the I½ teaspoons salt.

2. When the onions are almost done, add the greens to the boiling water and cook, uncovered, just until tender, about 2 minutes. Using tongs, lift the greens from the water, shake off the excess water, add them to the onions, and cook, stirring occasionally, until tender, about 5 minutes.

3. Using the same pot of boiling water, add the spaghetti and cook, stirring occasionally, until al dente, 8 to 10 minutes. Scoop out and reserve about I cup of the cooking water; drain the pasta. Transfer the pasta to a serving bowl and toss with the cheese. Add the greens and some of the reserved pasta water and toss, adding more water as necessary to keep the pasta from clumping. Scatter the garlic chips over the top and serve.

bowties with **cauliflower, olives & lemon** 4 servings

1 head cauliflower (about 2 pounds), cut into bite-size florets (about 8 cups)

¼ cup extra-virgin olive oil

5 cloves garlic, roughly chopped

¼ teaspoon crushed red pepper

2½ teaspoons kosher salt, plus additional for pasta water

12 ounces bowtie pasta (also called farfalle)

½ cup pitted kalamata olives, roughly chopped

1 teaspoon finely grated lemon zest

Freshly ground black pepper

GAME PLAN: Prepare and roast the cauliflower while the water comes to a boil. Chop the olives and zest the lemon while the pasta cooks.

1. Preheat the oven to 450°F. Bring a large pot of cold water to a boil over high heat. Toss the cauliflower with the olive oil, garlic, and red pepper on a baking sheet; sprinkle with 2 teaspoons of the salt and toss again. Roast until golden and tender, about 20 minutes.

2. Meanwhile, when the pasta water boils, salt it generously and add the bowties. Cook, stirring occasionally, until al dente, about 10 minutes. Scoop out ¼ cup of the pasta cooking water and set aside; drain the pasta. Return the pasta to the pot and toss with the cauliflower, reserved pasta water, the olives, lemon zest, remaining ½ teaspoon salt, and black pepper to taste.

STYLE Serving pasta in warmed pasta bowls is a professional touch. Place oven-safe bowls in a warm oven until you're ready to dish it out or warm the bowls by running them through your dishwasher's hot air cycle.

● pantry picks
● double duty
● real quick
● cool tools

Prep time: 15 minutes active time (plus 8 hours in the slow cooker)
Special equipment: Slow cooker

Why wait until the weekend to make a slow-simmered hearty braise or pasta sauce? A slow cooker makes weekday comfort cooking a hands-off proposition.

weekday italian gravy

6 servings, plus extra sauce

2 tablespoons extra-virgin olive oil

1½ pounds hot Italian-style link sausage

2 tablespoons tomato paste

½ cup water

4 pieces beef shank, each 1 inch thick (about 3½ pounds)

2 28-ounce cans crushed tomatoes

6 sun-dried tomatoes, preferably not oil-packed

1 large onion, chopped

6 cloves garlic, smashed

2 teaspoons dried Italian herb mix

1 bay leaf

1 tablespoon kosher salt

Freshly ground black pepper

1 pound tubular pasta, such as rigatoni or ziti

Freshly grated Parmesan or pecorino cheese

1. Heat a heavy skillet over medium-high heat. Add the oil and then the sausage; cook, turning occasionally, until brown all over, about 5 minutes. Transfer the sausage to the slow cooker. Pour off and discard all the oil in the skillet and return it to the heat. Add the tomato paste and cook, stirring, until brick red, about 1 minute. Add the water and bring to a boil, stirring to scrape up the browned bits. Pour the mixture over the sausage.

2. Add the beef shins, crushed tomatoes, sun-dried tomatoes, onion, garlic, Italian herbs, bay leaf, salt, and pepper to taste. Set the slow cooker on LOW for 8 hours, cover, and cook until the beef is very tender. Remove and discard bay leaf.

3. When ready to serve, bring a large pot of water to a boil and salt it generously. Add the pasta to the boiling water and cook, stirring occasionally, until al dente, about 10 minutes. Transfer the sausage and beef to a cutting board, slice into serving portions, and arrange on a serving platter. Drain the pasta and toss with some of the sauce; transfer to a serving bowl. Serve the meat and pasta separately with sauce on the side. Freeze any leftover sauce for up to 3 months.

KNOW-HOW Uncover the essence of tomatoes fast by cooking the tomato paste to concentrate its flavor before adding liquid to the pan.

singapore **fried** rice

4 to 6 servings

¼ cup vegetable oil

8 ounces ham or smoked chicken or turkey, diced

Kosher salt

Freshly ground black pepper

3 cloves garlic

1 2-inch piece peeled fresh ginger

1 bunch scallions (white and green parts kept separate), thinly sliced

1 heaping cup frozen corn, peas, or carrots, or a mix

3 large eggs, lightly beaten

1 tablespoon hot Madras curry powder

4 cups cold cooked jasmine rice

1. Heat a large nonstick skillet over high heat. Add 1 tablespoon of the oil, then add the ham or other meats. Season with salt and pepper to taste and stir-fry until browned, about 2 minutes.

2. While the ham browns, finely chop the garlic and ginger together in a mini-chopper. Add the mixture to the ham, along with the scallion whites, and stir-fry until fragrant, about 30 seconds. Add the frozen vegetables, season with salt and pepper to taste, and stir-fry until vegetables are heated but still crisp, about 1 minute. Transfer the mixture to a large serving bowl.

3. Return the skillet to the heat and add 1 tablespoon of the oil. Add eggs and season with salt and pepper to taste. Cook, stirring constantly, until eggs are set but still tender. Tip eggs out of the pan into the bowl with the ham mixture and break eggs up with a wooden spoon or spatula.

4. Return the skillet to the heat and add the remaining 2 tablespoons oil and the curry powder. Stir until fragrant, about 30 seconds. Add the rice to the pan, breaking up any clumps, and stir-fry until coated evenly with the oil. Cook the rice undisturbed until the bottom is slightly crisp, about 3 to 4 minutes. Stir scallion greens into the rice. Add rice to the serving bowl, stir to distribute the ingredients evenly, and season with salt and pepper to taste.

When ordering Asian takeout tonight, think outside the box and stock up for tomorrow's stir-fry. Give extra rice a spicy spin with on-hand items such as curry powder or chile oil.

● pantry pride

● poultry party

● real quick

● cool tools

Prep time: 35 minutes
Special equipment: pressure cooker

Winter root vegetables add a creamy sweetness to risotto that leaves spring vegetables green with envy.

risotto with winter vegetables
4 servings

- 4 tablespoons unsalted butter
- I medium onion, chopped
- 4 cloves garlic, smashed
- I teaspoon kosher salt, plus additional for seasoning

  Freshly ground black pepper
- I½ cups Arborio rice
- 3 carrots, cut into large chunks
- 2 sprigs fresh thyme
- I small celery root (about I pound), peeled and cut into chunks
- I butternut squash, halved, peeled, seeded, and cut into large chunks (optional)
- 3 cups chicken broth, low-sodium canned or homemade
- ½ cup dry white wine
- I large bunch mustard greens, washed and torn (4 to 5 cups)
- I cup freshly grated pecorino cheese, plus additional for serving

GAME PLAN: Cut the carrots and celery root while the onions and garlic saute. Tear and wash the greens while the risotto cooks.

I. Melt 2 tablespoons of the butter in a 7-liter pressure cooker over medium-high heat. Add the onion, garlic, the I teaspoon salt, and the pepper to taste and cook, stirring occasionally, until the vegetables soften a bit, about 5 minutes. Add the rice and stir to coat. Stir in the carrots, thyme sprigs, celery root, squash (if desired), chicken broth, and wine. Close the pressure cooker lid and bring the pressure up to high (which can take up to IO minutes), then reduce the heat to maintain an even pressure for 3 minutes. Remove from the heat and gently press the cooker's pressure indicator stem until no more steam comes out (this may take up to 2 minutes—see the operating tips on page 2I9).

2. Carefully remove the lid—the risotto will look a bit soupy at this point. Stir the mustard greens into the risotto, then let the mixture sit until the greens wilt, about 2 minutes. Stir in the remaining 2 tablespoons butter and the I cup cheese. Season to taste with salt and pepper, if you like. Pass additional grated cheese at the table.

SHOPSMART Squash your prep time by buying peeled, seeded, and chopped butternut squash from your supermarket.

We love making risotto, but the last thing we want to do when we get home from a long workday is babysit a pot of rice. We wondered if a pressure cooker's high heat and concentrated steam could do the work for us. It was worth a shot.

shrimp & saffron **risotto**

4 servings

2 tablespoons extra-virgin olive oil

1 small onion, coarsley chopped

3 large cloves garlic, smashed

1 teaspoon fennel seeds

1 teaspoon kosher salt, plus additional for seasoning

Freshly ground black pepper

1½ cups Arborio rice

2 tablespoons tomato paste

Pinch saffron threads

¼ cup dry white vermouth

3 cups chicken broth, low-sodium canned or homemade

1 pound medium shrimp, peeled and deveined

1. Heat the olive oil in a 7-liter pressure cooker over medium-high heat. Add the onion, garlic, fennel seeds, the 1 teaspoon salt, and pepper to taste. Cook, stirring occasionally, until the vegetables soften a bit, about 5 minutes. Add the rice, tomato paste, and saffron and stir until the grains are evenly colored. Stir in vermouth and chicken broth. Close the pressure cooker lid and bring the pressure up to high (which can take up to 10 minutes), then reduce the heat, if necessary, to maintain an even pressure for 3 minutes. Remove from the heat and gently press the cooker's pressure indicator stem until no more steam comes out. (This may take up to 2 minutes—see operating tips on page 219.)

2. Carefully remove the lid—the risotto will look a bit soupy at this point. Stir in the shrimp and let the risotto stand, off the heat, until shrimp are pale pink and cooked through, about 2 minutes. Season with additional salt and pepper to taste.

real quick

Prep time: 30 minutes

This is the perfect one-pot summer supper, garden fresh with a balance of cool, fast flavor.

beef & **bulgur pilaf** with mint

4 servings

4 tablespoons extra-virgin olive oil

¼ cup pine nuts

8 ounces lean ground beef

¼ teaspoon ground allspice

1½ cups medium-grain bulgur

3½ cups chicken broth, low-sodium canned

1 medium zucchini, diced

1½ teaspoons kosher salt

Freshly ground black pepper

2 cups cherry or grape tomatoes

2 scallions (green and white parts)

¼ cup chopped fresh dill

¼ cup fresh mint, coarsely chopped

1 clove garlic, minced

Finely grated zest and freshly squeezed juice of ½ lemon (about 2 tablespoons juice)

GAME PLAN: Prep the cherry tomatoes, scallions, and the rest of the salad while the bulgur cooks.

1. Heat 2 tablespoons of the olive oil and the pine nuts in a Dutch oven or soup pot over medium-high heat and stir occasionally until the nuts are toasted, about 2 minutes. Add the ground beef, breaking it up with a spoon. Sprinkle with the allspice and cook, stirring, until the meat is no longer pink, about 3 minutes. Stir in the bulgur and cook until lightly toasted, about 3 minutes. Add the chicken broth, bring the mixture to a boil, and then adjust the heat to maintain a gentle simmer. Scatter the zucchini over the surface of the pilaf (don't stir it in; it will steam on top) and sprinkle with 1 teaspoon of the salt and pepper to taste. Cook, uncovered, until the bulgur is tender but not mushy, 10 to 12 minutes.

2. Meanwhile, halve the tomatoes and thinly slice the scallions. Toss them with the dill, mint, garlic, lemon zest and juice, the remaining 2 tablespoons olive oil, the remaining ½ teaspoon salt, and pepper to taste.

3. Mound the pilaf on a serving platter and spoon the tomato salad evenly over the top. Serve warm.

SHOPSMART Bulgur is quick-cooking cracked wheat that's most often used in the Middle Eastern side dish tabbouleh. We take advantage of its chewy charm and healthy fiber content in our pilaf.

● **pantry picks**

● double duty

● real quick

● cool tools

Prep time: 45 minutes

Why save bread pudding for dessert when it's great dressed for dinner? Our skillet cornbread pudding jacks up this comfy classic with ease.

skillet cornbread pudding with ham & pepper jack 4 to 6 servings

2 tablespoons unsalted butter

1½ cups cooked corn, thawed frozen or fresh

1 bunch scallions (white and green parts), sliced

1 6-ounce chunk Black Forest ham, diced (about 1¼ cups)

1 clove garlic, chopped

½ teaspoon chili powder

3 large eggs

2 cups half-and-half

4 ounces pepper Jack cheese, diced

¼ cup chopped fresh basil

1 teaspoon kosher salt

Freshly ground black pepper

1 cup packaged cornbread stuffing cubes

Pinch sugar

1. Preheat the oven to 350°F. Melt the butter in a 10-inch cast-iron skillet over medium heat. Add the corn, scallions, ham, garlic, and chili powder. Cook, stirring occasionally, until the scallions are soft, about 3 minutes. Meanwhile, lightly beat the eggs in a large bowl and stir in the half-and-half, cheese, basil, salt, and pepper to taste.

2. Pull the skillet from the heat. Stir the cornbread stuffing and sugar into the skillet. Pour the egg mixture over and stir gently to distribute all the ingredients evenly. Transfer the skillet to the oven and bake until lightly puffed and golden, about 30 minutes. Serve warm.

STYLE Lightly dressed mesclun mounded next to a serving of savory bread pudding transforms this country skillet dish from down-home to downtown.

indoor-grilled salmon with fennel & orange • grilled salmon with peppers & herbs • moroccan-spiced grouper with celery • grilled tuna with napa slaw & wasabi mayo • grilled trout in grape leaves • sole gratin with tomatoes, capers & olives • steamed sea bass with citrus & herbs • thai shrimp curry • shrimp & lettuce stir-fry • mussels with tomatoes, basil & saffron

fish &
seafood

Fish dinners reel
in easy elegance
with little effort.

● pantry picks

● double duty

● real quick

● cool tools

Prep time: 20 minutes

Our fennel and orange salad is great any time, but we especially like it in winter. Fresh, bright, and lively, it takes only minutes to make and is guaranteed to chase away the winter blahs.

indoor-grilled **salmon with fennel** & orange 4 servings

SALAD

½ medium red onion, thinly sliced

¾ teaspoon kosher salt, plus additional for seasoning

2 medium fennel bulbs (about 1½ pounds), trimmed and halved through the core

2 to 3 tablespoons basil-flavored olive oil

1 tablespoon white wine vinegar

2 navel oranges

Freshly ground black pepper

SALMON

4 5-ounce center-cut salmon fillets (about 1 inch thick)

2 tablespoons olive oil

Kosher salt

Freshly ground black pepper

3 tablespoons dry English-style mustard

3 tablespoons honey

1 tablespoon water

KNOW-HOW For crisscross grill marks, give the salmon a quarter turn when it's halfway cooked on each side.

GAME PLAN: Let the salmon come to room temperature while the onion soaks. Make the mustard mixture while the salmon grills on its first side.

1. Preheat the oven to 450°F. For the salad: Soak the onion in salted ice water for 10 minutes. Meanwhile, thinly slice the fennel lengthwise, using a mandoline if you have one. Put the fennel in a serving bowl and toss with the ¾ teaspoon salt, olive oil, and vinegar. Trim all of the peel and white pith from the oranges, halve them top to bottom, and slice into thin half-moons. Add the oranges to the fennel. Drain the onion, pat dry, and add it to the salad; season with salt and pepper to taste and toss.

2. For the salmon: Heat a grill pan or cast-iron skillet over medium-high heat. Brush the salmon lightly with the olive oil and season both sides with salt and pepper to taste. Lay the fillets skin side up in the pan and grill for 5 minutes.

3. Meanwhile, make the Honey-Mustard Sauce: Whisk mustard, honey, and water in a small bowl until smooth. Turn the salmon over, brush generously with the sauce, and transfer the grill pan to the oven. Bake the fish 2 to 3 minutes if you like it pink, or 5 minutes for fish that is cooked through but still moist.

4. Transfer salmon to a platter and let it rest for a couple minutes to finish cooking. Serve with the fennel salad.

We love grilling in packages. So simple, colorful, and healthful— perfect after a full day on the set.

grilled salmon with peppers & herbs 4 servings

1 red onion, halved and very thinly sliced

1 celery heart, with leaves, very thinly sliced

1 red or yellow bell pepper, halved, seeded, and thinly sliced

3 tablespoons extra-virgin olive oil

1 teaspoon kosher salt

Freshly ground black pepper

2 sprigs fresh rosemary

1 lemon, very thinly sliced

1½ pounds center-cut skinless salmon fillet, in 1 piece

1. Heat an outdoor grill to medium. Mound the onion, celery, and bell pepper down the center of a 24x18-inch piece of heavy-duty aluminum foil (or double a piece of regular aluminum foil to make a 24x18-inch piece). Drizzle with olive oil and toss; season with the salt and black pepper to taste, and toss again. Spread the vegetables out to make an even bed for the fish. Lay rosemary sprigs and all but 4 of the lemon slices on top. Season the salmon with salt and black pepper to taste and lay it skin side down on the vegetables. Top the salmon with the reserved lemon slices. Bring the edges of the foil up and crimp them closed to make a package, leaving a bit of room for the steam inside to circulate around the fish.

2. Place the packet on the grill and cook for 10 minutes. Carefully open the foil and insert an instant-read thermometer in the thickest part of the fillet. The thermometer should register 120°F to 125°F. If it is a few degrees under, reseal and cook for 2 to 3 minutes more. Remove it from the grill and let rest for 5 to 10 minutes to finish cooking. It's this gentle "carryover cooking" off the heat that gives the fish its wonderful, moist texture.

3. Cut the salmon into 4 equal pieces and transfer to plates. Spoon some of the vegetables and the collected juices over each portion and serve.

SHOPSMART Protected by outer stalks, the heart of a celery bunch comprises the most tender, slender ribs.

moroccan-spiced grouper
with celery 4 servings

4   ribs celery, preferably with
    leaves

1   cinnamon stick

1   teaspoon ground coriander

1   teaspoon sweet paprika

¾   teaspoon ground ginger

    Pinch cayenne pepper

1   small onion, halved and sliced

1   cup water

¼   cup extra-virgin olive oil

2   cloves garlic, smashed

1¼ teaspoons kosher salt, plus
    additional for seasoning

6   canned plum tomatoes, drained

4   8-ounce grouper or other thick
    white-fleshed fish fillets

    Grilled naan or other flatbread,
    for serving (optional)

I. Split the celery ribs lengthwise and cut into 2-inch pieces; roughly chop the leaves, if available. Toast the cinnamon stick, coriander, paprika, ginger, and cayenne in a dry medium skillet over medium-high heat until fragrant, about 30 seconds. Add the celery, onion, water, olive oil, garlic, and 1¼ teaspoons salt. Bring to a boil, cover, reduce the heat to maintain a simmer, and cook just until the celery is tender, about 6 minutes.

2. Crush the tomatoes through your fingers into the skillet and stir. Season the fillets with salt to taste and nestle them in the vegetables. Cover and simmer gently just until the fish is cooked through but not flaking, 6 to 8 minutes.

3. Divide the fish among 4 shallow bowls. Bring the sauce to a boil and cook until thickened slightly, about 4 minutes. Spoon the sauce over and around the fish and serve with grilled flatbread, if desired.

KNOW-HOW If you're waiting for fish to flake before taking it off the heat, you're waiting too long. Once it turns opaque from top to bottom, it's good to go—remember that it'll continue to cook from residual heat after you remove it from the pan.

Toast your spices to muscle up the flavor of everything from sauces to stews and pilafs. The heady perfume that fills the kitchen is aromatherapy for your appetite.

grilled tuna with napa slaw & wasabi mayo

4 servings

WASABI MAYONNAISE

- 4 teaspoons wasabi powder
- 4 teaspoons water
- ½ cup mayonnaise

SLAW AND TUNA

- ½ head (about 1 pound) napa cabbage, quartered, cored, and thinly sliced (6 cups)
- 6 ounces fresh snow or sugar snap peas, cut in thirds crosswise
- ¼ cup pickled ginger, drained and chopped
- 1½ teaspoons kosher salt, plus additional for tuna

  Freshly ground black pepper
- ¼ cup rice wine vinegar
- 2 tablespoons peanut oil, plus additional for tuna
- 1 1¼-pound tuna steak (about 2 inches thick)
- 2 teaspoons *gomashio* (Japanese sesame-seed spice blend) (optional) (See ShopSmart on page 64.)

1. Heat an outdoor grill or preheat a grill pan to medium-high. Whisk the wasabi and water in a small bowl to make a thick paste; turn the bowl over and set aside for a couple minutes. Whisk in the mayonnaise until smooth. Cover until ready to use.

2. For the slaw: Toss the cabbage, snow peas, pickled ginger, 1½ teaspoons salt, and pepper to taste in a large bowl. Add the vinegar and the 2 tablespoons peanut oil and toss again to coat.

3. For the tuna: Brush the tuna lightly all over with peanut oil and season generously with salt and pepper. Grill the tuna until it looks cooked about ⅓ inch up the side, about 3 minutes; then turn and cook another 3 minutes. Using tongs, hold the tuna on its sides to brown, about 1 minute on all sides. (If you like your fish medium, add 1 to 2 minutes per side to the cooking time.) Set aside for 5 minutes before cutting.

4. Cut the tuna into bite-size chunks. Mound some slaw on each of 4 plates and arrange the tuna on top. Sprinkle some *gomashio* over each serving, if desired, and serve with a dollop of wasabi mayonnaise.

SHOPSMART When buying tuna, ask for sushi-grade tuna, the highest quality available, and look for glossy, bright red steaks.

● luxury picks

● doable dish

● cool quick

● cool tools

Prep time: 35 minutes

This is fast, easy, and impressive. Don't be intimidated by the whole fish—this is the way fish are meant to be served.

grilled trout in grape leaves
4 servings

FISH

4 whole rainbow trout (each about 14 ounces)

Kosher salt

Freshly ground black pepper

2 tablespoons unsalted butter, diced

1 bunch fresh thyme sprigs

About 20 jarred grape leaves

Extra-virgin olive oil

VINAIGRETTE

1 lemon

1 tablespoon chopped fresh thyme

Kosher salt

Freshly ground black pepper

3 tablespoons extra-virgin olive oil

STYLE Cushion a platter with parsley and thyme, then lay the whole fish on their herb bed and surround them with lemon wedges.

1. For the fish: Heat an outdoor grill or preheat a grill pan to medium. Season the fish cavities with salt and pepper to taste. Stuff each fish with a quarter of the butter and thyme sprigs. Season the outside of the fish with salt and pepper to taste.

2. Rinse the grape leaves in a colander and pat them dry. Lay 3 leaves sideways and slightly overlapping on the work surface. Lay 2 more leaves along the far edge of the line of leaves to make a large sheet of grape leaves. Lay a fish across the leaves and wrap around the fish. Tie the fish in 2 or 3 places with kitchen twine. Repeat with the remaining fish and leaves.

3. Brush the wrapped fish lightly with oil. Grill the trout until an instant-read thermometer inserted into the thickest part of the fish registers 125°F, turning once, about 5 to 7 minutes per side. Set aside for 5 minutes before serving.

4. For the vinaigrette: Squeeze the lemon juice into a small bowl and stir in thyme and salt and pepper to taste. Gradually whisk in the oil to make a dressing. Snip off the string and serve each fish with a bit of the dressing.

Go fish! With barely any prep work and less than 15 minutes of cooking time, there's no denying that fish presents a swift solution to the daily question of what's for supper—and that's no fish tale.

GRILL IT IN 15 (or less)

• A medium-hot grill cooks fish perfectly—you're in the clear if you can hold your hand 5 inches above the grill grate for 5 seconds.

• A clean and hot grill grate **+** a fish that's been lightly oiled on both sides **=** no sticking.

• Make it even easier—grill fish in a foil package with vegetables, herbs, and slices of citrus or in a grill basket.

eamed Sea Bass with Citrus & Herbs

Sole Gratin with Tomatoes, Capers & Olives

Pan-seared scallops

STEAM IT IN 6

• No steamer? Try making one: Set a colander inside a wide pot, or place a small cooling rack inside a tall-sided skillet, then cover.

• For a shot of extra flavor, lay fish on a bed of citrus and herbs or spike the steaming liquid with chiles, gingerroot, or wine.

• Skewer raw shrimp or scallops on woody sprigs of rosemary or lemongrass.

BAKE IT IN 7
(minutes per inch)

• Follow this rule for fillets and you'll never go wrong: 7 minutes per inch of thickness in a 350°F oven.

• For a quick meal, coat fish with pesto or mustard, then press in seasoned breadcrumbs or panko and bake.

PAN-SEAR IT IN 8
(or less)

• Use a preheated pan to keep fish from sticking.

• Cook skin side up first and hang back until the fish tells you when to flip—it'll be opaque about two-thirds up from the bottom.

• Flip, then sear on side two just until cooked through. (It'll be opaque from top to bottom.)

Prep time: 30 minutes

Baked beneath a
blanket of golden
bread crumbs,
this is a fish dish
that flirts with the
Mediterranean
without venturing
too far
from home.

sole gratin with **tomatoes, capers & olives** 4 servings

5 tablespoons extra-virgin olive oil, plus additional for pan and fish

4 6-ounce fillets of sole

¼ teaspoon kosher salt, plus additional for seasoning

Freshly ground black pepper

4 to 5 canned plum tomatoes, drained

1 small onion, halved and sliced

4 to 5 pitted kalamata olives, chopped

1 heaping teaspoon capers, drained

½ cup flat-leaf parsley, coarsely chopped

¼ cup dried bread crumbs

1. Preheat the oven to 400°F. Lightly brush a 1½-quart oval gratin dish with olive oil. Lay the fish out on the work surface skin side up, drizzle with a bit of the oil, and season with some salt and pepper to taste. Fold the fillets in half (thick end over thin) and lay the pieces down the center of the prepared pan, slightly overlapping.

2. Crush the tomatoes through your fingers into a small bowl. Stir in 3 tablespoons of the olive oil, the onion, olives, capers, the ¼ teaspoon salt, and pepper to taste. Stir in the parsley and spoon the mixture over the fish.

3. Toss remaining 2 tablespoons olive oil with the bread crumbs until evenly moistened and scatter them over the fish. Bake until the fish is cooked through and the crumbs get crispy and brown, about 25 minutes.

KNOW-HOW Can you tell which end is up? Let the herringbone pattern be your clue—this is the skin side, so keep it facing up and center.

steamed sea bass with citrus & herbs

6 servings

Perfumed in a steam bath of citrus and herbs, this light fish dish is a welcome reward after a taxing day.

1 medium bunch fresh herbs such as dill, parsley, thyme, tarragon, or a mix

1 lemon

1 lime

1 small orange

4 6-ounce sea bass or red snapper fillets

¼ cup extra-virgin olive oil

½ teaspoon kosher salt, plus additional for seasoning

Freshly ground black pepper

SHOPSMART Black sea bass (not the Chilean kind) and red snapper both have the delicate and flaky texture that allows the fish to steam quickly.

1. Chop enough herbs to make ¼ cup and set aside. Finely grate about 1 teaspoon zest from each citrus fruit and add to the chopped herbs. Pour an inch or more of water in a wok or skillet and bring to a boil over medium-high heat.

2. Make a bed of the remaining whole herbs in a bamboo or collapsible steamer and cover with 3 or 4 slices of each citrus fruit (reserve the remaining lemon and lime halves for juice). Lay 2 of the fish fillets skin side down on top of the herbs, drizzle with some of the oil, and season with some salt and pepper to taste. Place the 2 remaining fillets skin side up on top of the other fillets (see photo on page 89). Set the steamer over the water, cover, and cook for 10 minutes or just until the fish is barely cooked through. Turn off the heat and leave fish covered in the steamer over the hot water for 5 more minutes to finish cooking.

3. Meanwhile, squeeze about 1 tablespoon each of juice from the lemon and lime into a medium bowl. Season with the ½ teaspoon salt and pepper to taste. Gradually whisk in the remaining olive oil, starting with a few drops and then adding the rest in a steady stream to make a smooth dressing. Stir in the reserved herbs and zest.

4. Divide the fish among 4 plates, discarding the whole herbs and citrus slices, and drizzle some dressing over the fish. Pass extra dressing at the table.

thai **shrimp** curry

4 servings

2   tablespoons peanut oil

1   pound medium shrimp, peeled, deveined, and tails removed

1   13½-ounce can unsweetened coconut milk

2   teaspoons prepared Thai red curry paste

1   stalk lemongrass, sliced (see page 31)

1   tablespoon fish sauce

2   teaspoons dark brown sugar

1   teaspoon kosher salt

8   ears canned baby corn (about ½ can)

4   scallions (white and green parts), chopped

½   cup sliced canned water chestnuts, drained

½   cup canned straw mushrooms, drained

¼   cup fresh basil leaves, torn

2   tablespoons torn mint leaves

1   lime

    Hot cooked jasmine rice

    Sliced scallions (white and green parts) (optional)

1. Heat the oil in a large skillet over medium-high heat. Add the shrimp and stir-fry just until pink and curled but not cooked through, about 2 minutes. Transfer the shrimp to a plate and set aside.

2. Skim the thick cream from the surface of the coconut milk and add it to the skillet along with the curry paste. Cook, stirring, until smooth and fragrant and a bit shiny, about 1 minute. Stir in the remaining coconut milk, the lemongrass, fish sauce, brown sugar, and salt; simmer for 3 minutes, uncovered. Return the shrimp to the skillet along with the baby corn, scallions, water chestnuts, and straw mushrooms. Simmer until the shrimp finish cooking, about 3 minutes more. Pull the pan off the heat. Stir in the basil and mint, and squeeze in the lime's juice. Serve with jasmine rice. Sprinkle with sliced scallions, if desired.

SHOPSMART We love Thai curry pastes. Based on chiles along with other spices, prepared pastes are used in tandem with liquid—usually coconut milk—to tame their spiciness. Buy them in a jar or can in any hue—red, yellow, or green. They're all instant flavor boosters.

● pantry picks
● double duty
● **real quick**
● cool tools

Prep time: 25 minutes

There's no
denying that
iceberg lettuce is
this year's
comeback kid.
Besides its retro
salad appeal, it
stands up to heat
and stays crisp
under fire—both
key for stir-fry.

shrimp & lettuce stir-fry
4 servings

1½ pounds large shrimp, peeled,
      deveined, tails removed

2 tablespoons cornstarch

1 tablespoon soy sauce

1 tablespoon dark sesame oil

1 tablespoon Shaohsing rice
      cooking wine or pale dry sherry

1 tablespoon sugar

1 teaspoon crushed red pepper

½ teaspoon kosher salt, plus
      additional for seasoning

1 tablespoon water

3 scallions

3 cloves garlic

1 1-inch piece fresh ginger, peeled

1 head iceberg lettuce (about
      1¼ pounds)

3 tablespoons vegetable oil

   Hot cooked jasmine rice

**SHOPSMART There are many
varieties of Chinese rice wine, but we
like to use Shaohsing, one of the
higher-quality versions. If you can't
find it, use sherry.**

GAME PLAN: Have all of your ingredients, sauces, and
seasonings portioned out and ready to go.

1. Toss shrimp with 1 tablespoon of the cornstarch, the soy
sauce, sesame oil, rice wine, sugar, crushed red pepper,
and the ½ teaspoon salt in a medium bowl. Set aside for 10
minutes.

2. Meanwhile, mix the remaining 1 tablespoon cornstarch
with the water. Slice the scallions diagonally, keeping
whites and greens separate. Mince the garlic and ginger in
a minichopper. Quarter and core the head of lettuce, then
halve each quarter, rinse, and pat dry. Toss with about half
the ginger mixture.

3. Heat a large skillet over high heat. Heat 2 tablespoons of
the oil, then add the shrimp and stir-fry until they are
opaque and halfway cooked, about 2 minutes. Add the
remaining ginger mixture and the scallion whites and
continue to stir-fry until the shrimp are pink and just firm,
1 to 2 minutes. Transfer the shrimp to a plate.

4. Return skillet to the heat and add remaining 1 tablespoon
oil. Add lettuce and a generous pinch of salt and toss until
the leaves wilt slightly. Return the shrimp to the pan with
most of the scallion greens and toss. Add the cornstarch
mixture, bring to a boil, and boil just until the sauce
thickens. Transfer to a large platter, scatter the remaining
scallion greens over the top, and serve with hot rice.

mussels with tomatoes, basil & saffron

4 servings

Put that silverware down and eat mussels like a pro: Use an empty shell like a tong to pluck the mussel from its shell.

¼ cup extra-virgin olive oil

2 shallots, thinly sliced

6 cloves garlic, smashed

1 28-ounce can whole tomatoes, drained and roughly chopped

1 orange

1 cup dry white vermouth or dry white wine

Large pinch saffron threads

5 pounds mussels, scrubbed and debearded

2 slightly heaping cups fresh basil, roughly chopped

1. Heat the olive oil in a large pot or Dutch oven over medium-high heat. Add the shallots and garlic and cook, stirring, until the garlic is golden, 3 to 4 minutes. Add the tomatoes and cook until almost dry, about 3 minutes. Use a swivel peeler to peel off 2 long strips of zest from the orange and add them to the pot. Squeeze the orange's juice into the tomatoes, then stir in the vermouth and saffron. Raise the heat to high and bring the mixture to a rapid boil.

2. Add the mussels. Cover and cook, shaking the pot once or twice, just until they begin to open, 3 to 4 minutes. Stir in the basil and cook until most mussels open, about 2 minutes more. Spoon the mussels into large warm serving bowls and ladle some of the broth over each serving. Discard any mussels that didn't open.

STYLE Be sure to serve a basket of crusty bread for soaking up the delicious broth.

chicken saltimbocca • chicken with tomatoes & pepperoncini • smothered chicken with onions • chicken-in-a-pot • chicken breasts with balsamic & garlic • chicken with leeks, watercress & radish • grilled chicken with avocado cucumber salad • north african chicken stew • philippine chicken adobo • caribbean chicken pepper pot • chicken fingers with apricot sauce • crispy falafel chicken with yogurt salad • roast turkey • turkey enchilada casserole • turkey hoppin' john • turkey turnovers • 30-minute turkey chili

poultry

Our inspiring
takes on
winged cuisine
encourage plain
poultry to
take flight.

● pantry picks

● double duty

● real quick

● cook books

Prep time: 35 minutes

This easy twist on the classic veal dish is a total winner. Guests love it, and it impresses with minimal effort.

chicken saltimbocca

4 servings

Instant flour for dredging, such as Wondra

4 boneless, skinless chicken breast halves (about I to 1½ pounds)

Freshly ground black pepper

16 fresh sage leaves

4 thin slices prosciutto (about 2 ounces)

I tablespoon extra-virgin olive oil

I tablespoon unsalted butter

5 ounces cremini mushrooms, sliced

2 cloves garlic, smashed

½ cup dry Marsala wine

3 tablespoons water

⅓ cup crème fraîche

2 tablespoons chopped fresh flat-leaf parsley (optional)

Kosher salt

I. Preheat the oven to 375°F. Put the flour in a shallow dish. Lay the chicken breasts smooth side up on a piece of waxed paper and season lightly with pepper. Lay 3 sage leaves across the top of each chicken breast and then wrap with a slice of prosciutto, tucking the ends of the prosciutto underneath. Heat a large skillet over medium-high heat; add the oil and butter. Dredge the wrapped chicken in the flour, shaking off excess. Place the chicken in the pan with the prosciutto seam side down and cook, turning once, until lightly browned on both sides, about 5 minutes in all. Transfer the chicken to a roasting pan and bake, uncovered, for IO minutes.

2. Turn the heat under the skillet to high. Add the mushrooms and garlic and cook, stirring, until the mushrooms brown, about 4 minutes. Add the Marsala and the remaining 4 sage leaves and bring to a boil, scraping up any browned bits with a wooden spoon; cook until the liquid is almost gone. Add the water, pull the pan off the heat, and swirl in the crème fraîche and parsley, if using. Season the sauce with salt and black pepper to taste. Pool the mushroom sauce on individual plates or on a serving platter and arrange the chicken pieces on top.

SHOPSMART Crème fraîche is a cultured cream—sort of a rich yogurt. It's perfect for adding luster to sauces in a flash. If you can't find it, add heavy cream stirred with a drop or two of lemon juice.

chicken with tomatoes
& pepperoncini 4 servings

2 tablespoons extra-virgin olive oil

4 bone-in chicken breast halves, with skin (about 2½ to 3 pounds)

½ teaspoon kosher salt, plus additional for seasoning

Freshly ground black pepper

2 medium shallots, thinly sliced

2 cloves garlic, chopped

4 cups canned crushed tomatoes

I cup chicken broth, low-sodium canned or homemade

8 jarred pepperoncini

1½ tablespoons capers, rinsed and drained

¼ cup chopped fresh basil

Fresh basil leaves (optional)

GAME PLAN: Prep the shallots, garlic, capers, and basil while the chicken breasts cook.

I. Preheat the oven to 425°F. Heat a large skillet over medium-high heat; add olive oil. Pat the chicken dry and season the skin side with some salt and black pepper to taste. Lay the chicken seasoned side down in the skillet and brown well; transfer the chicken to a casserole dish and put in the oven.

2. While the chicken bakes, turn the heat under the skillet to medium, add the shallots, and cook, stirring occasionally, until they begin to soften. Stir in the garlic and cook until fragrant (about 30 seconds), then add the tomatoes, broth, pepperoncini, capers, and the ½ teaspoon salt; bring to a simmer. Stir in about half the chopped basil and pour the sauce into the casserole dish, taking care not to pour it over browned chicken skin. Bake 10 to 15 minutes more or until an instant-read thermometer registers 170°F when inserted in the thickest part of the breasts. Stir in remaining basil. Put a chicken breast on each of four dinner plates and spoon on some sauce. Sprinkle with basil leaves, if desired.

KNOW-HOW For the best flavor, brown all sides of the meat. Hard-to-sear spots like ends and edges are best tackled with tongs—use them to stand pieces on end and prop meat or poultry on its side to brown.

● **pantry picks**

● double duty

● real quick

● cool tools

Prep time: 20 minutes

Soulful smothered chicken is a classic southern country-style dish that can be thrown together in 20 minutes and satisfies everyone at the table.

smothered chicken with onions 4 servings

3   tablespoons vegetable oil

Kosher salt

Freshly ground black pepper

4   boneless, skinless chicken breast halves (about 1 to 1½ pounds)

1   medium onion, halved and sliced

2   sprigs fresh thyme, plus additional sprigs for garnish

2   tablespoons all-purpose flour

2   tablespoons unsalted butter, softened

½   cup dry white vermouth or white wine

1⅔ cups chicken broth

1   tablespoon whole-grain mustard (optional)

KNOW-HOW We like to use beurre manié, a paste made from equal parts of butter and flour to thicken sauces. Just add it to the saucepan, bring to a boil, and watch it transform a thin sauce to a creamy one.

GAME PLAN: Slice the onion while the chicken browns. Blend the butter and flour while the onions cook.

1. Preheat the oven to 400°F. Heat a large skillet over medium-high heat; add 2 tablespoons of the oil. Season the chicken with salt and pepper to taste. Lay the chicken skinned side down in the skillet and cook until golden, about 4 minutes per side. Transfer the chicken to a baking dish or roasting pan and bake just until firm to the touch, about 10 minutes.

2. Meanwhile, increase the heat under the skillet to high. Add the remaining 1 tablespoon oil, the onion, and 2 sprigs thyme and season with salt and pepper to taste. Cook, stirring occasionally, until the onion browns, about 5 minutes. While the onion cooks, work the flour and butter together in a small bowl with a fork to make a paste.

3. Add the vermouth to the skillet and stir with a wooden spoon to scrape up the browned bits from the bottom of the pan. Simmer until the wine is reduced by about half, then add the broth and bring the mixture to a full boil. Whisk in the flour mixture a bit at a time and bring the liquid back to a full boil. Simmer until the sauce thickens, about 1 minute more. Whisk in the mustard, if using, and season with salt and pepper. Pour the sauce over the chicken, garnish with thyme sprigs, and serve.

pantry picks

double duty

really quick

cool tools

Prep time: 25 minutes
Special equipment: pressure cooker

chicken-in-a-pot
4 servings

Last-minute
chicken soup
doesn't have to
confine you to
instant or canned
varieties. Through
the magic of
pressure cooking,
homemade
chicken soup *fast*
is a reality.

6 large carrots, peeled and cut into 1/2-inch chunks

2 large onions, halved and thinly sliced

4 long strips lemon zest

4 sprigs fresh dill, plus 2 tablespoons chopped

2 tablespoons extra-virgin olive oil

1/2 teaspoon kosher salt, plus additional for seasoning

4 bone-in chicken breast halves, skin removed (2 1/2 to 3 pounds)

2 cups chicken broth

I. Put the carrots, onions, lemon zest, dill sprigs, and olive oil in a 7-liter pressure cooker. Season the vegetables with the 1/2 teaspoon salt and the chicken with salt to taste. Pour the broth in the pot, then nestle the chicken meat side down on top of the vegetables. Close the pressure cooker lid; bring the pressure up to high (this can take up to 10 minutes). Adjust the heat, if necessary, to maintain an even high pressure for 10 minutes. Remove from the heat and use the quick-release method to bring down the pressure (see operating tips, page 219).

2. Stir the chopped dill into the chicken stew. Put I chicken breast in each of 4 large soup bowls and ladle some carrots and broth over each one.

KNOW-HOW Boneless, skinless chicken breasts are fast—but when we want melt-in-your-mouth texture and a hearty flavor, we opt for chicken cooked on the bone.

Party on the fly!

Just because you're the one throwing the party doesn't mean you can't enjoy it. Here's a Friday after-work menu that gets appetizers, dinner, and dessert on the table without your even breaking a sweat.

6:00 PM. Dress the set: Preheat your oven to 450°F. Chill your wine (if it needs it), put on some fun music and an apron, and get cooking! Start with Citrus-Spiced Olives.

6:30 PM. Make the tiramisù: Soak ladyfingers, fold together mascarpone cream, assemble, and chill. Put cheese out to warm up to room temperature. Prep and roast zucchini (it's fantastic when served at room temp).

menu

Citrus-spiced olives, cheese, crusty bread & roasted nuts • chicken saltimbocca • polenta • roasted zucchini with herbs • tiramisù rapido

INSIDER SECRETS

We asked our Food Network colleagues for some of their tried-and-true party tips.

• Always start a party with a clean kitchen and an empty dishwasher.

• Keep hors d'oeuvres simple—olives, crackers and cheese, and cheese straws are all great and simple starters.

• Make dessert ahead of time.

• Don't be afraid to delegate. Take people up on their "Can I bring anything?" offer. Request dishes that go with what you're serving as the main event, such as appetizers, bread, or dessert.

7:00 PM. Chop and roll: Once the zucchini's done, turn down the oven to 375°F. Slice mushrooms and chop parsley and herbs for chicken and zucchini. Roll chicken with prosciutto and sage, and chill. Grate cheese for polenta.

7:30 PM. Set the stage: Put out skillet for chicken along with other cooking tools and serving platters. Cut bread (or ask an early-arriving guest to do the honor) that goes with the cheese and olives. Prepare polenta; cover and keep warm. Have a glass of wine and wait for your guests to arrive.

Prep time: 30 minutes

Like a best friend, this chicken dinner is always dependable. Made from pantry ingredients, it deserves to be called upon often.

chicken breasts with
balsamic & garlic 4 servings

2 tablespoons vegetable oil

Kosher salt

Freshly ground black pepper

4 boneless, skinless chicken breast halves (about 2 pounds)

2 tablespoons all-purpose flour

2 tablespoons unsalted butter, softened

5 cloves garlic, smashed

1 sprig rosemary, plus 4 additional sprigs for garnish (optional)

$1/3$ cup balsamic vinegar

$1^2/3$ cups chicken broth

1. Preheat the oven to 350°F. Heat a large skillet over medium-high heat; add the oil. Pat the chicken dry and season with salt and pepper to taste. Lay the breast halves smooth side down in the skillet and cook, turning once, until golden, about 4 minutes per side. While the chicken cooks, work the flour and butter together in a small bowl with a fork to make a paste. Transfer the chicken to a baking dish and bake for 10 to 12 minutes while you make the sauce.

2. Add the garlic and 1 sprig rosemary to the skillet over medium-high heat and toss to toast slightly, about 1 minute. Stir in the vinegar, scraping the browned bits from the bottom of the pan, and simmer until vinegar begins to thicken and coats the pan, about 1 minute. Add the chicken broth and bring to a boil. Whisk in the flour mixture a bit at a time and bring the mixture back to a full boil. Simmer until the sauce thickens, about 1 minute more. Season with salt and pepper to taste. Put the chicken on a platter, pour the sauce over, and garnish with the remaining rosemary sprigs, if desired. (Shown with Glazed Radishes, page 163.)

SHOPSMART We cook with inexpensive deep-purple balsamic vinegar—not white balsamic. Its harmonious balance of sweet-tangy flavor and inky color effortlessly beefs up sauces and marinades.

chicken with leeks,
watercress & radish 4 servings

Enliven your repertoire any season with this refreshing all-in-one chicken dish.

3 tablespoons vegetable oil

4 bone-in chicken breast halves, with skin (about 2½ to 3 pounds)

½ teaspoon kosher salt, plus additional for seasoning

Freshly ground black pepper

4 tablespoons unsalted butter

2 leeks (white and light green parts), halved lengthwise, sliced crosswise, and rinsed

4 radishes, thinly sliced into rounds

¼ cup dry white vermouth

⅓ cup heavy cream

1 bunch watercress, stems trimmed (reserve a few sprigs for garnish), roughly chopped

GAME PLAN: Slice and clean the leeks while pan-searing the chicken.

1. Preheat the oven to 350°F. Heat a large skillet over medium-high heat; add the oil. Pat the chicken dry and season with some salt and pepper to taste. Lay the chicken skin side down in the skillet and cook undisturbed until the skin is golden and crispy, about 4 minutes. Add a nut-size bit of the butter to the skillet, and when the butter smells fragrant, turn the chicken and cook until opaque, about 4 minutes more. Put the chicken in a baking dish or roasting pan and bake just until firm to the touch, 10 to 12 minutes.

2. Pour all but 1 tablespoon fat from the skillet and return pan to the heat. Add the leeks and radishes and cook, tossing, until wilted, about 4 minutes. Season with the ½ teaspoon salt and pepper to taste. Add the vermouth, bring to a boil, and reduce until syrupy. Stir in the cream and bring to a boil. Remove the skillet from the heat, add the watercress, and toss just until it is wilted. Add the remaining butter and swirl the skillet until it melts. Stir in any chicken juices that have collected in the roasting pan. Spoon the leek mixture onto 4 plates and arrange the chicken breasts on top. Garnish with the reserved watercress sprigs and serve.

KNOW-HOW Quick-clean leeks by slicing in half lengthwise, then cutting crosswise. Place in a colander set into a big bowl of cool water. Swish sand and dirt free and lift out.

● pantry picks

● double duty

● real quick

● cool tools

Prep time: 20 minutes

Fire up the grill,
watch the sunset,
and rediscover
why it's called the
great outdoors.

grilled chicken with avocado
cucumber salad 4 servings

CHICKEN

4   chicken paillards, about
    6 ounces each (see Know-How,
    below)

    Extra-virgin olive oil

1   teaspoon ground coriander

    Kosher salt

    Freshly ground black pepper

SALAD

1   kirby cucumber with peel,
    coarsely chopped

1   cup grape or cherry tomatoes
    and/or yellow pear tomatoes,
    halved

¼   red onion, diced

1   tablespoon chopped fresh
    tarragon

1   teaspoon grated lemon zest
    (about ½ lemon)

    Freshly squeezed juice of half a
    lemon (1 to 2 tablespoons)

½   teaspoon kosher salt

    Pinch cayenne pepper

1   ripe Hass avocado

GAME PLAN: Make the salad while grilling the chicken.

1. For the chicken: Preheat a grill pan or heat an outdoor grill to medium-high. Brush the chicken paillards lightly with olive oil and season with the coriander, salt, and black pepper to taste. Grill the chicken, in batches if necessary to avoid crowding the pan, turning once, until cooked through, about 2 minutes per side.

2. For the salad: While the chicken cooks, toss the cucumber, tomatoes, onion, tarragon, lemon zest and juice, salt, and cayenne pepper in a serving bowl. Halve the avocado; press a knife into the pit, twist, and lift out. Score the flesh with the tip of a knife, and then use a spoon to scoop it from the skins and into the salad; toss gently to combine. Put a paillard on each of 4 plates and spoon some salad over the chicken.

KNOW-HOW To butterfly chicken breasts for paillards: Turn the breast over and pull away the tenderloin. Flip over and slice into two halves horizontally, leaving the far edge intact. Open the breast. Using the flat side of your chef's knife, pound chicken (as you would smash a garlic clove) so that it is of an even thickness. This is called a paillard.

Finished with a flourish of our Tunisian Pesto, this heady dish satisfies an appetite for quick exotic comfort.

north african chicken stew

4 servings

1½ cups chicken broth

 1 cup uncooked couscous

 4 teaspoons kosher salt

  Freshly ground black pepper

 1 tablespoon vegetable oil

 1 tablespoon unsalted butter

 6 boneless, skinless chicken thighs, quartered (about 1¼ pounds)

 1 teaspoon ground cumin

 1 teaspoon paprika, preferably Spanish pimenton (smoked paprika)

 2 carrots, sliced ¼ inch thick

 1 small red onion, halved and sliced

1⅔ cups chicken broth

 ¼ cup apple cider vinegar

  Grated zest of 1 lemon

 ⅓ cup Tunisian Pesto (see page 14)

1. Bring the 1½ cups chicken broth to a boil in a medium saucepan over high heat. Stir in the couscous, 1 teaspoon of the salt, and pepper to taste. Cover and set aside while you make the stew.

2. Heat the oil and butter in a Dutch oven. Season the chicken with the remaining salt, cumin, paprika, and pepper to taste; add to the pot. Cook, stirring occasionally, until browned all over, about 5 minutes. Add the carrots, onion, the 1⅔ cups chicken broth, vinegar, and lemon zest; bring to a boil. Adjust the heat to maintain a brisk simmer, cover, and cook just until the chicken is firm to the touch and the carrots are tender, about 8 minutes.

3. Stir the pesto into the stew. Fluff the couscous with a fork and mound it in 4 soup bowls. Spoon some chicken stew over each portion and serve.

SHOPSMART Couscous is small granular-shape pasta made from crushed and steamed semolina. It's incredibly quick-cooking and practically effortless to make.

philippine chicken adobo

4 servings

3 tablespoons vegetable oil
(or half butter and half oil)

8 skinless, bone-in chicken thighs
(about 2¾ pounds)

1 teaspoon kosher salt, plus
additional for seasoning

15 cloves garlic, smashed

2 bay leaves

2 cups water

¾ cup distilled white vinegar

2 tablespoons soy sauce

1 tablespoon sugar

¾ teaspoon coarsely ground black
pepper

¼ teaspoon crushed red pepper

1 tablespoon cornstarch mixed
with 1 tablespoon cold water

Hot cooked rice, for serving
(optional)

1. Heat a large skillet over medium-high heat. Add the oil (or oil and butter, if using). Pat chicken dry and season with some salt to taste. Add the chicken smooth side down and cook until brown, about 4 minutes. Scatter the garlic and bay leaves around the chicken, then add the water, vinegar, soy sauce, sugar, the 1 teaspoon salt, black pepper, and red pepper. Bring the liquid to a boil; adjust heat to maintain a simmer. Cook, uncovered, turning the chicken occasionally, until tender, about 25 minutes.

2. Transfer the chicken to a bowl. Remove and discard bay leaves. Whisk the cornstarch mixture into sauce and simmer, whisking constantly, until it thickens a bit. Return the chicken and any juices to the sauce and simmer gently, turning the chicken occasionally, until it is very tender and glazed, about 10 minutes more. Serve over rice, if desired.

KNOW-HOW Rather than chopping, breeze through 15 cloves of garlic in no time by smashing them with the flat side of your knife.

caribbean chicken pepper pot
6 servings

Cocktails with paper umbrellas are for tourists. Those in the know go for this devilishly spicy Caribbean Pepper Pot instead.

¼ cup vegetable oil

1 medium onion, halved and sliced

2 bay leaves

1½ tablespoons kosher salt, plus additional for seasoning

2 teaspoons ground allspice

1 heaping teaspoon dried thyme

⅓ cup tomato paste

Freshly ground black pepper

8 skinless, bone-in chicken thighs (about 2½ pounds)

3½ cups water

1 Scotch bonnet chile, pierced (if you like it really hot, mince it)

8 ounces fresh okra, trimmed, halved crosswise

3 thick sweet potatoes (about 2 pounds), each cut into 4 rounds with skin on

1 bunch collard greens (about 1 pound), stems removed, chopped

1. Heat a 7-liter pressure cooker over medium heat. Stir in the oil, onion, bay leaves, 1½ tablespoons salt, the allspice, and thyme; cook, uncovered, until soft, about 8 minutes. Increase the heat to high, stir in the tomato paste, and cook, stirring and scraping, until it turns brick red, about 2 minutes.

2. Season the chicken with some salt and black pepper to taste and add it to the pot, turning to coat with the tomato and onion. Stir in the water, then add the chile, okra, potatoes, and collard greens in that order. You don't need to stir—the collards will cook down and keep everything moist as the cooker comes up to pressure. Close the pressure cooker lid and bring the pressure up to high (which can take up to 10 minutes), then reduce the heat, if necessary, to maintain an even pressure for 7 minutes. Remove from the heat and gently press the pressure indicator stem until no more steam comes out (see quick-release method operating tip, page 219). Carefully open the pot. Remove and discard bay leaves. Ladle the stew into bowls and serve.

COOK'S NOTE Not for the faint of heart, Scotch bonnets are about as fiery as a chile gets. If you can't find one, substitute a habanero.

These chicken fingers feed more than just the K-12 crowd. Made from meaty chicken breasts, our juicy fingers will have you licking your digits clean.

chicken fingers with apricot sauce 4 servings

CHICKEN

4   boneless, skinless chicken breast halves (about 1½ pounds)

2   cups panko (Japanese coarse bread crumbs)

2   teaspoons finely grated lemon zest

2   teaspoons kosher salt, plus additional for seasoning

3   large eggs

Vegetable oil for frying

Freshly ground black pepper

1   lemon, cut into wedges

SAUCE

Makes 1 cup

⅔   cup apricot preserves

2   tablespoons soy sauce

2   teaspoons ketchup

6   slices unpeeled fresh ginger

Freshly squeezed juice from half a lemon (about 2 tablespoons)

GAME PLAN: So it has time to cool, microwave the sauce before starting the chicken.

1. Set a rack on a baking sheet, put it in the oven, and preheat to 200°F. Cut each chicken breast into 4 thick, even pieces. Toss the panko, lemon zest, and 2 teaspoons salt in a shallow bowl or pie plate. Beat the eggs lightly in another.

2. Heat about ½ inch oil in a large, heavy skillet over medium-high heat. Season the chicken all over with salt and pepper to taste, dip in the eggs, and then press into the panko mixture to coat evenly, shaking off any excess. Carefully place the chicken in the hot oil, taking care not to crowd the pan. Adjust the heat as necessary to maintain a constant sizzle. Fry the chicken, a few pieces at a time, turning once, until evenly brown, about 5 minutes total. Keep cooked fingers warm in the oven on the rack. Repeat with the rest of the chicken. Serve the chicken hot with lemon wedges and the dipping sauce.

APRICOT SAUCE

Combine the preserves, soy sauce, ketchup, and ginger in a small microwave-safe bowl. Cover with plastic wrap and microwave on HIGH until the preserves melt, about 30 seconds. Stir in lemon juice and cool before serving.

COOK'S NOTE Panko bread crumbs are our top choice for coating pan-fried cutlets, fish, and vegetables. The coating stays crisp and browns beautifully.

crispy falafel chicken with yogurt salad 4 servings

Dip, shake, and fry your way to the Middle East. Preseasoned with exotic spices, falafel mix adds a fresh coat of crunch to chicken.

CHICKEN

½ cup prepared falafel mix

Vegetable oil for frying

4 boneless, skinless chicken breast halves, tenders removed (about 1½ pounds)

Kosher salt

Freshly ground black pepper

SALAD

3 kirby cucumbers, diced

¼ cup fresh mint leaves, roughly torn

¼ cup fresh dill fronds, coarsely chopped

¼ red onion, diced (about ½ cup)

1 small clove garlic, minced

1½ teaspoons kosher salt

1 lemon

½ cup plain whole-milk yogurt

GAME PLAN: Make the salad while the chicken bakes.

1. For the chicken: Preheat the oven to 400°F. Place a small rack on a baking sheet. Put the falafel mix in a pie plate or other shallow bowl. Heat about ½ inch oil in a large, heavy skillet over medium-high heat. Season the chicken breasts with salt and black pepper to taste and coat with the falafel mix, shaking off any excess. Carefully place the chicken smooth side down in the hot oil, taking care not to crowd the pan. Cook until nicely browned, turning once, 2 to 3 minutes per side. Repeat with the rest of the chicken. Transfer the chicken to the prepared rack. Bake until firm but slightly springy when pressed, 6 to 8 minutes.

2. Meanwhile, make the Yogurt Salad: Toss the mint, cucumbers, dill, onion, garlic, and salt in a small bowl. Finely grate the zest from the lemon into the salad and squeeze in the lemon's juice too. Stir the yogurt into the salad.

3. Arrange chicken on a platter and serve with salad or put a chicken breast on each of 4 plates with the salad.

COOK'S NOTE Don't toss those chicken tenders! Save them and thread on skewers for kabobs, pan-fry for burritos, or stir-fry.

Grill boneless, skinless chicken breasts for a quick dinner.

Vamping them up is a cinch with a simple sauce. Here are 12 of our favorites. Match these sauces with other grilled meats too.

squeeze

- Honey-Mustard Sauce (pictured; see recipe, page 80)

- Tunisian Pesto (see recipe, page 14)

- Peanut Sauce (see recipe, page 63)

dip

- Fresh Green Chutney (pictured, left; see recipe, page 16)

- Apple-Horseradish Sauce (see recipe, page 145)

- Apricot Sauce (see recipe, page 118)

mop

- Chipotle-Maple Mop Sauce (pictured, left; see recipe, page 147)

- Your favorite barbecue sauce

- Chile Oil (see recipe, page 19)

dollop

- Jamaican Papaya Salsa (pictured; see recipe, page 150)

- Yogurt Salad (see recipe, page 121)

- Tomato-Scallion Relish (see recipe, page 135)

● pantry picks

● **double duty**

● real quick

● cool tools

Prep time: 10 minutes active time; 3 hours roasting time

roast turkey

8 to 10 servings

What's fast and easy about roasting a turkey? The leftovers! A big bird cooked on the weekend provides the base for weekday meals. This is cooking smart.

1   8- to 10-pound turkey, neck and giblets removed

Kosher salt

Freshly ground black pepper

1   medium onion, quartered

1   head garlic, halved

Several sprigs of fresh herbs, such as thyme, parsley, rosemary, or sage

2   bay leaves

8   tablespoons unsalted butter, melted

1. Adjust a rack to lowest position and remove other racks. Preheat oven to 325°F. Dry bird well with paper towels inside and out. Season the inside of the breast cavity with salt and pepper to taste and stuff with the onion, garlic, herbs, and bay leaves. Set the bird on a roasting rack in a roasting pan breast side up and brush generously with half the butter and season again with salt and pepper to taste. Tent bird with aluminum foil.

2. Roast turkey for 2 hours. Remove the foil and baste with remaining butter and some of the pan drippings. Increase oven temperature to 425°F and continue to roast until an instant-read thermometer registers 170°F in the thigh of the bird, about 45 minutes more. Remove turkey from the oven and set aside to rest 20 minutes. Before carving, remove and discard onion, garlic, herbs, and bay leaves.

KNOW-HOW It is best to remove the breast meat, legs, and wings from the carcass before storing. Cut through the wing joints and reserve the first two joints; save the tips for broth. Remove each side of the breast in one piece by cutting straight along the top of the breast and then down along the rib bones. Pull legs back and away from the carcass and cut along the thigh to free them from the frame. Store turkey, tightly covered, for 3 to 4 days in the refrigerator. If freezing, store the pieces in broth in resealable plastic bags. Use the bones for turkey broth.

● pantry picks
● **double duty**
● rev-quick
● cool tools

Prep time: 40 minutes

Bold, bright
flavors celebrate
south-of-the-
border style. A
dollop of sour
cream and a
sprinkling of
cilantro add
creamy
freshness. A
margarita seals
the deal.

turkey **enchilada** casserole

4 servings

2 tablespoons vegetable oil

1 tablespoon unsalted butter

1 small onion, roughly chopped

2 cloves garlic, roughly chopped

1 jalapeño pepper, seeded and
   minced

1 slightly heaping teaspoon
   ground cumin

   Kosher salt

3 7-ounce cans tomatillo sauce

8 6-inch corn tortillas, preferably
   white, cut into quarters

2 cups cooked turkey meat, in
   bite-size pieces (about
   10 ounces)

1 15½-ounce can black beans,
   rinsed and drained

2 cups shredded cheddar or
   Monterey Jack cheese or a mix

   Sour cream (optional)

   Chopped fresh cilantro
   (optional)

I. Preheat the oven to 375°F. Heat the oil and butter in a large ovenproof skillet over medium heat. Add the onion, garlic, jalapeño, cumin, and salt to taste and cook until tender and fragrant, about 8 minutes. Stir in the tomatillo sauce, tortillas, turkey, and beans. Bring to a boil and stir in half the cheese.

2. Scatter the remaining cheese over the top and bake until casserole is bubbling and cheese has melted, about 20 minutes. Serve with sour cream and cilantro, if desired.

SHOPSMART If you're faced with the decision of buying yellow or white corn tortillas, always opt for the white ones. They taste better, have a less cottony texture, and are more pliable.

126

turkey hoppin' john
6 servings

6 slices bacon (about 4 ounces)

1 bunch scallions, sliced (white and green parts kept separate)

1 rib celery, sliced

4 cloves garlic, smashed

2 teaspoons kosher salt, plus additional for seasoning

1 teaspoon freshly ground black pepper, plus additional for seasoning

1 cup Southern long grain rice such as pecan, popcorn, or Texas basmati

6 cups chicken broth, low-sodium canned

2 cups roughly torn cooked dark-meat turkey

1 10-ounce package frozen black-eyed peas, thawed

1 bay leaf

2 tablespoons apple cider vinegar

GAME PLAN: Chop the scallions and shred the turkey while the bacon cooks.

1. Preheat the oven to 350°F. Crisp the bacon in a Dutch oven over medium-high heat, about 7 minutes. Remove the bacon, crumble it coarsely, and set aside; leave the pot over the heat.

2. Add the scallion whites, celery, garlic, 2 teaspoons salt, and 1 teaspoon pepper to the bacon fat in the pot and cook until tender and fragrant, 3 to 4 minutes. Stir in the rice. Raise the heat to high and stir in the chicken broth, turkey, black-eyed peas, bay leaf, and bacon. Bring the mixture to a boil, cover, and transfer to the oven. Bake until the rice is tender but not mushy, about 20 minutes.

3. Remove rice from the oven and let it rest 5 minutes— don't open the pot. Remove and discard bay leaf. Stir in the cider vinegar, adjust the seasonings, and scatter the scallion greens over the top.

SHOPSMART For the biggest, freshest flavor, use aromatic long grain basmati rice hybrids such as pecan (also called popcorn) or Texmati and frozen black-eyed peas instead of canned.

Some believe that eating Hoppin' John on New Year's Day will bring you luck all year long. If you associate good fortune with eating good food, you've hit pay dirt.

It's easy cooking green. It's never been simpler to eat your veggies—especially with savvy supermarkets offering presliced, washed, and packed-to-go vegetables for cooks on the run.

raw

Easiest of all is eating them au naturel. Here are some of our favorite vegetables in the rough:

- Sliced fennel
- Jicama sticks
- Sliced broccoli stems
- Grated carrots
- Chopped celery root

prep

Make double and save yourself trouble.

- Chop extra onions, scallions, and garlic; bag and use within a couple of days.

- Roasting veggies? Make twice as much and use leftovers in a panini, an omelet, or a salad.

- Two heads of broccoli are better than one. Steam an extra head and use in a hash or pilaf.

zap

No pots to clean. No cooktop space to sacrifice. No reason not to love your microwave. Just cover and cook.

- Corn: 2 minutes/ear
- Asparagus: 4 minutes/pound
- Artichokes: 7 minutes/I large
- Winter squash: 7 minutes/pound
- Beets: I2 minutes/pound

ease

Put your supermarket to work for you.

Hit the salad bar, a great resource for prechopped and sliced veggies for stir-frying.

Cruise the produce aisles for sliced mushrooms, peeled garlic cloves, and washed salad greens.

Grab a prefab soup bag (with soup mix, cut vegetables, etc.), dismantle, and use the vegetables.

mushrooms with rosemary & garlic

4 servings

Mushrooms are the ultimate fall guy. They're always available and, when roasted, always delicious.

1½ pounds mixed fresh mushrooms, such as shiitake, cremini, or oyster, trimmed and cleaned

6 garlic cloves, smashed

3 sprigs fresh rosemary

½ cup extra-virgin olive oil

1½ teaspoons kosher salt, plus additional for seasoning (optional)

Freshly ground black pepper

¼ cup water

1. Preheat the oven to 450°F. Toss the mushrooms, garlic, and rosemary with the olive oil in a shallow baking pan. Season with the 1½ teaspoon salt and pepper to taste and toss again. Roast the mushrooms until golden, 20 to 25 minutes. Stir in the water, scraping up the brown bits on the bottom of the pan and tossing until the mushrooms are glazed. Season with more salt, if desired, and serve warm or at room temperature.

KNOW-HOW Never wash mushrooms. Wipe or brush dirt off with a paper towel or mushroom brush. Shiitake stems are too tough to eat, so they must be removed. Cremini and oyster stems are fine left on.

● **pantry picks**

● double duty

● real quick

● cool tools

Prep time: 30 minutes

We love this rustic Italian-style side with our Peppered Beef Tenderloin with Merlot and Blue-Cheese Smashed Potatoes.

braised fennel

4 servings

2 medium bulbs fennel, tops trimmed

¼ cup extra-virgin olive oil

¼ cup dry white vermouth

½ teaspoon kosher salt

½ teaspoon fennel or anise seeds (optional)

Freshly ground black pepper

½ cup water

I. Cut each fennel bulb through the core into 6 even wedges. Put the wedges in a large skillet with the olive oil, vermouth, salt, fennel seeds (if using), and the pepper to taste. Add enough water to come about halfway up the sides of the fennel. Bring the mixture to a boil over medium-high heat.

2. Cut a circle of parchment paper the size of the pan and lay it over the fennel. Reduce the heat to maintain a gentle simmer and cook the fennel, turning once about halfway through cooking, until tender, about 25 minutes.

3. Serve immediately or remove the parchment, increase the heat to high, and cook until all of the liquid evaporates and the fennel browns, about 8 minutes more.

KNOW-HOW The more the fennel cooks, the more it will caramelize, so feel free to take it beyond our suggested cooking time. This technique also works for onions, carrots, and parsnips.

American grits
and Italian
polenta provide
delicious comfort
for both cook
and company.

cheesy grits
4 servings

2 cups chicken broth

2 cups milk

¾ cup old-fashioned grits

1 sprig fresh thyme

1 tablespoon unsalted butter

½ teaspoon kosher salt

   Pinch cayenne pepper

1 cup grated cheddar cheese or
   ½ cup grated pecorino cheese

Stir the chicken broth, milk, grits, thyme, butter, salt, and cayenne pepper in a large microwave-safe bowl or glass measuring cup. Microwave on HIGH, uncovered, for 12 minutes and then stir. Grits should be fairly thick but still moist—they will thicken more once you add the cheese. If they still seem too loose, microwave up to another 3 minutes. Remove the thyme sprig from the grits, stir in the cheese, and serve hot. (Shown with Polenta, page 176.)

SHOPSMART Flavor and texture always outrank speed. That's why we choose old-fashioned grits over the quick-cooking variety.

● **pantry picks**

● double duty

● real quick

● cool tools

Prep time: 20 minutes

Polenta takes on many forms and flavors. Leave out the cheese and black pepper and serve it for breakfast with maple syrup.

polenta

4 to 6 servings

2 cups chicken broth

2 cups whole milk

¾ cup quick-cooking polenta

¼ to ½ cup freshly grated Parmesan cheese

2 tablespoons unsalted butter, cut into bits

½ teaspoon kosher salt

Freshly ground black pepper

I. Put the broth and milk in a medium saucepan and bring to a boil over high heat. Slowly whisk in the polenta, reduce the heat to low, and cook, whisking occasionally, until the polenta is thick and creamy, about 15 minutes.

2. Pull the saucepan from the heat and whisk in the cheese, butter, salt, and pepper to taste. Serve immediately. (Pictured on page 175.)

COOK'S NOTE To make polenta cakes to use as a side dish or as a base for hors d'oeuvres, spread the warm polenta in a 13x9-inch baking dish, chill, cut, then grill in a grill pan or on an outdoor grill.

real quick

Prep time: 25 minutes

saucy orzo with summer squash

4 servings

2 teaspoons kosher salt, plus additional for seasoning

2 cups orzo

2 tablespoons extra-virgin olive oil

6 scallions (white and green parts kept separate), chopped

I medium zucchini, diced

I medium summer squash, diced

2 to 2½ cups chicken broth, vegetable broth, or water

¼ cup chopped fresh flat-leaf parsley

2 tablespoons chopped fresh dill

Freshly ground black pepper

1½ cups finely crumbled feta cheese (about 6 ounces)

I. Bring a medium saucepan of water to a boil over high heat, then salt it generously. Stir in the orzo and cook, stirring occasionally, until al dente, about 8 minutes; drain.

2. While the orzo cooks, heat the olive oil in a large skillet over medium heat. Add the scallion whites, zucchini, and summer squash and cook, uncovered, stirring occasionally, until all are tender, about 5 minutes. Stir in the orzo, broth, scallion greens, parsley, dill, the 2 teaspoons salt, and some pepper to taste. Simmer, uncovered, until the mixture thickens slightly, about 3 minutes. Stir in the feta cheese and serve.

SHOPSMART Orzo pasta resembles grains of rice. Try it in a brothy soup or in place of rice in a stuffing.

Pasta in rice's clothing? Orzo deserves top-shelf billing in your pantry. Use it as a playful alternative to rice in salads, sides, and pilafs.

Clockwise from top: Bacon Smashed Potatoes, Horseradish & Sour Cream Smashed Potatoes, Sun-dried Tomato Smashed Potatoes, Pesto Smashed Potatoes

smashed potatoes
4 servings

Play with your food. Smashed potatoes are the perfect vehicle for boldly flavored add-ins. These are a few of our favorites, but feel free to experiment with the condiments you like best.

2 pounds medium red-skinned potatoes, scrubbed

2 whole garlic cloves (optional)

1 sprig fresh thyme or rosemary (optional)

1/2 cup chicken broth or 3/4 cup milk

2 tablespoons extra-virgin olive oil or unsalted butter

2 teaspoons kosher salt, plus additional for salting water

Freshly grated nutmeg

Freshly ground black pepper

1. Put the potatoes, garlic, and herbs, if using, in a medium saucepan, cover with cold water, and season liberally with salt. Bring to a simmer over medium heat and cook until the potatoes are very tender, about 20 minutes. Drain and discard the herb sprig, if using.

2. Heat the chicken broth or milk in a microwave-safe bowl in the microwave until hot, about 1 minute. With a potato masher or large fork, smash the potatoes into a chunky puree, adding the hot liquid as you do. Stir in the olive oil or butter and season with the 2 teaspoons salt, nutmeg, and pepper to taste.

COOK'S NOTE If you like your potatoes smashed with olive oil, then use chicken broth as the liquid. If you prefer the taste of butter, then opt for milk. Consider one of these add-ins:

FOR BROTH-BASED POTATOES:

1 tablespoon chipotle chiles *en adobo*

1/3 to 1/2 cup baba ghanoush or hummus

1/3 to 1/2 cup onion jam

1/4 to 1/3 cup truffle or other flavored oil (omit olive oil)

2 to 4 scallions, finely chopped

FOR THESE, OMIT OLIVE OIL AND ADD A COUPLE MORE TABLESPOONS BROTH:

1/2 cup pesto

1/2 cup sun-dried tomato tapenade

1/3 cup artichoke tapenade

FOR MILK-BASED POTATOES:

Crumbled bacon

2 to 3 teaspoons chopped fresh rosemary or thyme

2 tablespoons horseradish mixed with 2 tablespoons sour cream

1/2 to 2/3 cup crumbled blue cheese

2/3 cup freshly grated Parmesan cheese

basmati rice pilaf with apricots 4 servings

- ¼ cup chopped dried apricots
- 2 wide strips lemon zest
- 2 cups cold water
- 3 tablespoons unsalted butter
- 1 teaspoon garam masala (an Indian spice blend)
- 1 medium onion, diced
- 1¼ teaspoons kosher salt
- 1 cup basmati rice, lightly rinsed and drained
  Freshly ground black pepper
- ⅓ cup fresh mint leaves
- ¼ cup toasted unsalted pistachios or cashews

GAME PLAN: Toast the nuts while the rice cooks.

1. Put the apricots and lemon zest in the 2 cups of cold water. Melt the butter in a medium saucepan over medium heat, add the garam masala, and toast, stirring, until fragrant, about 1 minute. Add the onion and ¼ teaspoon of the salt and cook, stirring occasionally, until the onion is tender and translucent, about 6 minutes.

2. Stir in the rice and cook, stirring occasionally, until it begins to brown, about 4 minutes. Stir in the water along with the apricots, lemon zest, the remaining 1 teaspoon salt, and pepper to taste. Bring to a simmer. Reduce the heat to low, wrap a clean dish towel around the saucepan lid, and cover saucepan. Cook for 10 minutes, set aside for 5 minutes undisturbed, then remove lid and fluff with a fork. Mound the pilaf on a serving platter or in a shallow bowl, tear the mint over, and top with the nuts.

COOK'S NOTE Wrapping the lid with a dish towel keeps the steam in the pot, encourages the rice grains to stay separate, and absorbs condensation that would otherwise collect on the lid and drip back into the pan.

quick & easy berry tart • strawberry shortcut cake • summer berry tapioca trifle • ice cream sandwiches • hot fudge sauce • flower sugar cookies • coconut-lime pudding cake • little cheesecakes with strawberry sauce • 3 sweet twists • portuguese custard tartlets • quick & easy chocolate cake • brown sugar-glazed pears • chocolate malted panna cotta • tiramisù rapido

eight

sweets

Dessert for everyone and everyone for dessert. Our sweet endings are uncomplicated and delectable.

● party picks

● double duty

● **real quick**

● cool tools

Prep time: 30 minutes

This ethereal berry tart is the answer to last-minute dessert dilemmas.

quick & easy berry tart

4 to 6 servings

1	9¼x10-inch sheet puff pastry, thawed (about 9 ounces)
½	cup crème fraîche
⅓	cup confectioners' sugar, plus additional for garnish
	Zest and juice of half a lime
	Pinch fine salt
2	tablespoons jam or jelly (not preserves), such as apricot, currant, or apple
2	tablespoons water
2	cups fresh blueberries, raspberries, or a mixture

COOK'S NOTE Stick with smooth jams and jellies to use as a glaze and save chunky preserves for toast.

1. Preheat the oven to 425°F. Line a baking sheet with parchment paper. Put the puff pastry on a cutting board and trim and fold it as shown in the photos below.

2. Transfer the dough to the baking sheet and bake for 20 minutes. Using the tip of a sharp knife, cut into the bottom pastry along the inner edge of the top crust, taking care not to cut all the way through. Press the pastry bottom in the center to flatten—don't worry if the surface flakes and crumbles a bit. Cool to room temperature.

3. Combine the crème fraîche, the ⅓ cup confectioners' sugar, lime zest and juice, and salt in a small bowl until smooth. Put mounds of the mixture in the bottom of the cooled pastry shell. Use a small offset spatula or the back of a spoon to spread it evenly.

4. Combine jam and water in a small microwave-safe bowl and microwave on HIGH until glossy, about 1 minute; cool. Toss blueberries with glaze to coat. Add the raspberries and toss again very gently. Carefully mound the berries on top of the crème fraîche or arrange them in a decorative pattern. Dust with confectioners' sugar, if desired, and serve immediately or set aside for up to 30 minutes.

1. Fold one sheet of puff pastry in half to make a triangle. Trim away overlay.
2. Using a pastry wheel or sharp knife, cut a two-inch border into each outer edge of the triangle. Stop cutting when you get 1½ inches from the triangle's tip.

3. Unfold the triangle and, using a pastry brush, dab border with water. Pick up one separated corner of border and fold over to opposite corner, placing it just inside corner. Fold the other separated corner over and press down on border to adhere it to the base.

strawberry shortcut cake

8 servings

CAKE

- 1 cup all-purpose flour
- ¾ cup granulated sugar
- 1 teaspoon baking powder
- ½ teaspoon fine salt
- 4 tablespoons unsalted butter, melted
- 1 large egg, beaten
- ½ cup whole milk
- 1 teaspoon pure vanilla extract

STRAWBERRIES AND CREAM

- 2 pints strawberries
- 1 tablespoon granulated sugar
- 1 cup heavy cream
- 1 tablespoon confectioners' sugar
- ½ teaspoon pure vanilla extract

KNOW-HOW Cutting a cake into layers is easy as saw-spin-separate: Begin to saw the cake in half horizontally. Just before you reach the middle of the cake, give it a quarter turn. Continue to saw almost to the center, then give it another quarter turn and saw again until you reach your original point of entry. Saw completely through the cake's center and separate the layers.

1. For the cake: Preheat the oven to 375°F. Butter an 8-inch round cake pan, line it with parchment paper, butter the paper, and dust the pan lightly with flour.

2. Whisk the flour with the granulated sugar, baking powder, and salt in a medium bowl. Lightly whisk in the butter, egg, milk, and vanilla, just until smooth. Pour the batter into the prepared cake pan and bake until a toothpick inserted in the center comes out clean, about 25 minutes. Cool on a rack for 10 minutes, then turn it out of the pan, flip upright, and cool completely on the rack.

3. For the strawberries and cream: Set aside 1 pint of the best-looking whole berries for topping the cake. Hull and thinly slice the rest of the berries and toss with the granulated sugar. Set aside. Whip the cream with the confectioners' sugar and vanilla to soft peaks. Refrigerate until ready to use.

4. To assemble the cake: Cut the cake in half horizontally with a serrated knife. Place the bottom layer cut side up on a cake stand or serving plate. Drizzle the juices from the sliced berries over the cut sides of both halves. Fold a couple tablespoons of the whipped cream into the sliced berries and spread over the bottom layer. Top with the other piece of cake, cut side down. Spread the remaining whipped cream on the top of the cake and top the cake with the whole berries.

Prep time: 45 minutes

Tapioca is back! It's served on the hippest restaurants' menus—make space for it on yours. Relish this refreshing blast from the past by putting it in a trifle.

summer berry tapioca trifle
4 servings

2 cups fresh raspberries, blueberries, blackberries, sliced strawberries, or a mix

½ cup plus I tablespoon granulated sugar

¾ cup milk

I large egg

¼ cup quick-cooking tapioca

¼ teaspoon fine salt

I cup buttermilk

I teaspoon pure vanilla extract

8 ladyfingers

¾ cup heavy cream

2 tablespoons confectioners' sugar

2 teaspoons light rum

I. Toss the berries with the I tablespoon of granulated sugar and set aside. Whisk the ½ cup granulated sugar, the milk, egg, tapioca, and salt in a medium saucepan and set aside to plump the tapioca, about 5 minutes. Cook over medium heat, stirring occasionally, until the mixture boils, about 6 minutes. Pull saucepan from the heat and stir in buttermilk and vanilla.

2. Quarter the ladyfingers crosswise and set aside 12 rounded end pieces. Put 5 pieces in the bottom of each of 4 wine or parfait glasses; top with about ⅓ cup of berries and then a quarter of the tapioca mixture. Press 3 of the reserved ladyfinger pieces, rounded tip up, around the inside of each glass and into the tapioca. Cover loosely with plastic wrap and chill until set and quite cold, about I hour in the refrigerator or 30 minutes in the freezer. While the trifle chills, whip the cream to soft peaks; add the confectioners' sugar and rum and whip until the cream holds a slightly firm peak. Keep the cream and reserved berries refrigerated until ready to serve.

3. To serve, top each trifle with a dollop of whipped cream, then spoon on some of the reserved berries.

STYLE A trifle of ladyfingers simply layered in a goblet or flute with berries, tapioca, and whipped cream is one of the easiest desserts to pull off.

ice cream sandwiches
6 servings

Your favorite ice cream + two incredibly decadent cookies = an ice cream sandwich worth screaming for.

¼ cup all-purpose flour

¼ cup Dutch-process cocoa

¼ teaspoon fine salt

⅛ teaspoon baking powder

3 tablespoons unsalted butter, softened

1 tablespoon shortening

½ cup sugar

1 large egg, beaten

½ teaspoon pure vanilla extract

2 pints any flavor ice cream

1. Preheat the oven to 350°F. Line two baking sheets with parchment paper.

2. Whisk the flour with the cocoa, salt, and baking powder in a small bowl. In another bowl beat the butter, shortening, and sugar with a handheld electric mixer until fluffy. Add the egg and vanilla and beat until smooth. Stir in the flour mixture by hand to make a smooth dough.

3. Using 1 heaping tablespoon per cookie, drop 6 mounds of dough on each baking sheet, leaving a couple inches between each cookie. Bake for 15 minutes. (For even baking, rotate the pans from top to bottom and back to front about halfway through baking.) Using a spatula, transfer the cookies to a wire rack and cool completely.

4. Meanwhile, turn the ice cream pints on their sides and use a serrated knife to slice each through the container into 3 even rounds. Freeze the ice cream disks until ready to assemble the sandwiches.

5. To assemble: Peel the cardboard from the ice cream disks and sandwich each between two cookies. Serve immediately, or wrap individually in plastic wrap and freeze for up to 1 week.

COOK'S NOTE The bottoms of some ice cream containers have a little lip to them, so take that into consideration when you are cutting the disks.

1. While the cookies bake, turn ice cream pints on their sides and slice each container into three even rounds. 2. Freeze ice cream disks on a baking sheet until cookies are cool. 3. Peel the cardboard away from ice cream. 4. Sandwich each slab between two cookies.

Here's the scoop:

It just doesn't get any easier than ice cream. Whether you swathe yours in sauce, dunk it in soda, or spike it with liqueur, moving beyond the bowl has never been tastier.

SCOOPING WITH FLAIR

Scoop one kind of ice cream, then midway through the scoop, move to a second flavor and finish the motion. You get one ice cream ball swirled with two flavors.

Sundae Bar

FANCY FLOATS
Cook up nouveau soda fountain creations for dessert.

Try peach ice cream with cream soda, mango ice cream with ginger beer, or vanilla ice cream with orange soda.

Hot Fudge Sauce

Fancy Floats

HOT FUDGE SAUCE
Microwave I cup semisweet chocolate chips on HIGH, stirring occasionally, until melted, about I½ to 2 minutes. Stir in ⅔ cup sweetened condensed milk, ¼ cup light corn syrup, ½ teaspoon pure vanilla extract, and a pinch of salt until smooth. Serve warm or at room temperature.

NO-HOLDS-BARRED SUNDAE BAR
Hot Fudge Sauce (recipe, right) or Strawberry Sauce (page 198); whipped cream flavored with your favorite liqueur or extract; Sugar & Spice Palmiers (page 201); quickly sautéed berries or Brown Sugar-Glazed Pears (page 206); cut-out circles of Yellow Cake (page 187) or Quick & Easy Chocolate Cake (page 205); toasted coconut or nuts, chocolate curls; and candy, candy, candy!

TEMPTING TARTUFO
Scoop and freeze ice cream until it's nice and hard. Dip the ice cream into lukewarm melted chocolate, then freeze until semi-hard. Roll the chocolate-covered ice cream in chopped pistachios, shredded coconut, or chocolate shavings.

Tartuffo

flower sugar cookies
1 dozen

COOKIES

- 1 cup unsalted butter, slightly softened
- ½ cup light brown sugar
- 1 large egg
- 2 teaspoons pure vanilla extract
- 2 cups all-purpose flour, plus additional for rolling out dough
- ¼ teaspoon fine salt

ICING

- ¼ cup water
- 3 tablespoons egg white powder
- 2 cups confectioners' sugar

  Sprinkles, chocolate chips, candies, or colored sugars as desired

1. For the cookies: Beat the butter in a large bowl with a handheld mixer until fluffy. Scrape down the sides of the bowl, add brown sugar, and continue beating until light, 2 to 3 minutes. Add egg and vanilla extract, beating until smooth. Gradually add the 2 cups flour and salt while mixing slowly to make a rough dough. Press dough into a ball by hand. Lightly dust the cookie dough with flour and roll it between 2 pieces of waxed paper into a ¼-inch-thick disk. Slide the disk in the paper onto a cookie sheet and freeze until firm, about 20 minutes (or refrigerate about an hour).

2. Evenly space the racks in the oven and preheat to 350°F. Transfer the dough to the work surface and remove the top sheet of paper. Cut into cookies with a 4-inch flower or other decorative cutter and transfer them to a parchment-lined or nonstick baking sheet. Press excess dough together and roll and cut into cookies as well. Bake until cookies' edges are golden, about 20 minutes. Cool on a rack.

3. For the icing: Whisk the water and egg white powder in a medium bowl until foamy and smooth. Gradually whisk in the confectioners' sugar to make a smooth icing. Spread a layer of icing over the entire surface of the cookies (or just in the center, if desired) with the back of a teaspoon. Place sprinkles, chocolate chips, or candies in the center of the cookies. Let rest until the icing sets, about 30 minutes.

coconut-lime pudding cake

4 servings

A cake with a built-in sauce—how could you go wrong? Have the ingredients ready to go in your pantry to satisfy your sweet tooth any time.

2 tablespoons unsalted butter, softened, plus a bit for the pan

¾ cup granulated sugar

¼ cup all-purpose flour

3 large eggs at room temperature, separated

½ cup limeade concentrate, thawed

¾ cup canned unsweetened coconut milk

¼ teaspoon fine salt

Toasted coconut, for garnish (optional)

GAME PLAN: Start boiling the water when you turn the oven on so it's ready when the cake goes into the oven. Separate eggs while the lime concentrate thaws in the microwave.

1. Position a rack in the center of the oven and preheat to 325°F. Lightly butter a 1-quart gratin dish or 8-inch round cake pan and set it in a roasting pan.

2. Beat the 2 tablespoons butter with ½ cup sugar in a large bowl until creamy, using a handheld electric mixer. Beat in the flour, then the egg yolks, limeade concentrate, coconut milk, and salt. (For the airiest egg whites, clean the beaters thoroughly so none of this mixture is left on them.) In another medium bowl whip the egg whites until they form soft peaks. While whipping, slowly pour in the remaining ¼ cup granulated sugar and continue beating until the whites hold stiff, glossy peaks. Fold a quarter of the whites into the coconut-lime mixture, then fold in the remaining whites.

3. Pour the batter into the prepared baking dish and add enough boiling water to the roasting pan to come halfway up the side of the dish. Bake about 35 minutes or until the top of the pudding cake is slightly puffed and golden. Remove from the water bath and cool on a wire rack for 10 minutes; serve warm. Garnish each serving with toasted coconut, if desired.

KNOW-HOW Baking the cake in a water bath ensures that it will bake evenly and retain its luscious, saucy bottom.

pantry picks

double duty

real quick

cool tools

**Prep time: 20 minutes active time
(2 hours in the refrigerator)**

Individual cheesecakes are more than just cute—they're quick. Faster baking than a big cheesecake, these little guys are also good for those who never learned how to share.

little **cheesecakes** with strawberry sauce 6 servings

CHEESECAKES

10 chocolate graham crackers, broken

¼ cup semisweet chocolate chips

3 tablespoons unsalted butter, melted

1 pound cream cheese, softened

¾ cup sugar

2 large eggs, room temperature

2 teaspoons pure vanilla extract

1 teaspoon grated orange zest

SAUCE

1 cup frozen strawberries, thawed

2 tablespoons sugar

COOK'S NOTE To test for doneness, shake the pan a little. When the cheesecakes are mostly set but still shimmy slightly in the center, they're done. If they crack, don't worry—dress with strawberry sauce and no one will be the wiser.

GAME PLAN: Microwave cream cheese on HIGH for 15 seconds to bring to room temperature. Place eggs in a bowl of warm water to bring to room temperature.

1. For the cheesecakes: Preheat the oven to 325°F. Process the graham crackers and chocolate chips in a food processor until finely ground. Add the butter and pulse until the mixture is sandy and moist. Divide mixture evenly among 6 jumbo muffin cups, then press it evenly over the bottoms and about two-thirds of the way up the sides. Bake just until crusts are set, about 8 minutes.

2. In a clean food processor bowl pulse the cream cheese, sugar, eggs, vanilla, and orange zest until smooth. Divide the filling evenly among the muffin cups and bake until the rims are slightly puffed and the centers are almost set, about 30 minutes. Cool the cheesecakes in the cups on a rack, then refrigerate, uncovered, for at least 2 hours.

3. Meanwhile, for the sauce: In a food processor or a blender puree the strawberries with the sugar.

4. When you are ready to serve, run a small knife around the outside of the cheesecakes, then use the knife to gently lift them from their molds. Transfer cheesecakes to dessert plates. Spoon some sauce over each and serve.

3 **sweet twists**

servings vary

We just can't get enough of puff. Twist it, twirl it, fold it up—whether filled with savories or sweets, it's always savvy.

PINWHEELS

- 4 teaspoons granulated sugar
- 1 teaspoon ground cinnamon
- 1 9¼x10-inch sheet puff pastry, thawed (about 9 ounces)
- 1 tablespoon unsalted butter, melted
- 2 tablespoons ground chocolate or sweetened cocoa

TWISTS

- ¼ cup light brown sugar
- ¼ cup pecan halves
- ½ teaspoon cinnamon
- 1 9¼x10-inch sheet puff pastry, thawed (about 9 ounces)
- 1 large egg, beaten

PALMIERS

- ½ cup turbinado sugar
- 1 9¼x10-inch sheet puff pastry, thawed (about 9 ounces)
- 1 teaspoon pumpkin pie spice or ground ginger
- 1 large egg, beaten with 1 tablespoon water

Chocolate Cinnamon Pinwheels: Preheat oven to 375°F. Combine sugar and cinnamon. Lay pastry on a piece of parchment or waxed paper. Brush lightly with butter and scatter half the sugar mixture and all the chocolate over the surface. Starting from a long end, roll up dough tightly. Freeze 20 minutes. Slice into ½-inch-thick circles and lay on a parchment-lined baking sheet. Sprinkle remaining cinnamon sugar over tops. Bake until golden brown, about 22 minutes. Cool on a rack.

Cinnamon Pecan Twists: Combine sugar, pecans, and cinnamon in a minichopper and process until sandy. Line a baking sheet with parchment paper. Unfold pastry and brush with egg. Spread sugar mixture over pastry, then cut pastry into ½-inch-wide strips. Twist strips. Lay on pan, pushing ends down with your thumb. Freeze 10 to 15 minutes, until firm. Preheat oven to 400°F. Bake until golden, rotating pan halfway, 18 to 20 minutes. Cool on a rack.

Sugar & Spice Palmiers: See photos, below. After Step 3, brush with egg wash, fold one half over the other, and press firmly. Reserve sugar that didn't stick. Freeze roll until firm, about 10 minutes. Preheat oven to 400°F. Cut pastry into ½-inch-thick slices (see last photo, below). Lay on a parchment-lined baking sheet; sprinkle with reserved sugar. Bake until light brown, about 12 minutes. Turn over and bake until golden, 8 minutes more. Cool on a rack.

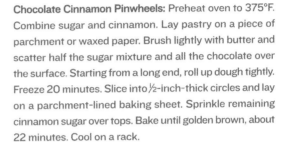

1. Sprinkle half of the sugar on a clean work surface and lay the puff pastry on top. Brush top of the pastry with the egg wash. 2. Sprinkle remaining sugar and spice on top. 3. Fold the edge of the pastry closest to you into the middle. Fold the other edge to the middle. Fold dough again to make 2 rolled-up sides.

● pantry picks

● ○○○

○

○

Prep time: 40 minutes

Move over, crème brûlée—there's a new custard in town. Fast and foolproof, these winning tartlets are our pick when we need to make a quick, impressive sweet.

portuguese custard tartlets

6 servings

| 9¼x10-inch sheet puff pastry, thawed (about 9 ounces)

4 large egg yolks

| cup heavy cream

½ cup sugar

| tablespoon cornstarch

Finely grated zest of ½ lemon

Pinch fine salt

COOK'S NOTE By thickening the custard on the stove top, we don't have to worry about the egg mixture curdling once we send it into the scorching 500°F oven.

I. Preheat the oven to 500°F. Roll and cut the puff pastry sheet as shown in the photos below. Put the pieces cut side up in 6 standard muffin cups, then wet your fingers with cold water and press the pastry over the bottoms and up the sides of the cups to make very thin shells—it's fine if they extend slightly over the rim. Freeze while you make the custard.

2. Whisk the egg yolks, cream, sugar, cornstarch, lemon zest, and salt in a medium saucepan. Heat over medium-high heat, whisking constantly, until the custard begins to thicken, about 6½ minutes. (That seems to be the magic time—at 6 minutes the custard is thin, and within the next 30 seconds it thickens just enough, like lemon curd. It does not need to boil.) Divide the custard evenly among the tartlet shells. Bake until the tops are slightly browned, about 15 minutes.

3. Cool 5 minutes in the pan on a rack, then unmold and cool completely before serving, about 30 minutes.

I. Roll I sheet of puff pastry into a tight coil. Cut coil into I½-inch pieces.
2. Place pieces in a standard muffin cup, then with a wet thumb, press piece down into cup.
3. Wet your fingers and gently push pastry up sides of muffin cup to make a thin shell.

quick & **easy chocolate** cake
6 servings

8 tablespoons unsalted butter

½ cup freshly brewed coffee

¼ cup unsweetened Dutch-process cocoa

l cup all-purpose flour

l cup granulated sugar

¼ teaspoon baking powder

¼ teaspoon fine salt

⅛ teaspoon baking soda

¼ cup sour cream

l large egg, room temperature

½ teaspoon pure vanilla extract

Confectioners' sugar for dusting

Ice cream or sweetened whipped cream, for serving (optional)

l. Preheat the oven to 350°F. Butter a 9-inch round cake pan, line bottom with a round of parchment paper, then lightly butter the paper.

2. Put the butter, coffee, and cocoa in a microwave-safe bowl, cover with plastic wrap, and microwave on HIGH until the butter melts, about 2 minutes. Whisk to combine.

3. Meanwhile, whisk the flour, granulated sugar, baking powder, salt, and baking soda in a large bowl. Beat the sour cream with the egg and vanilla in a small bowl. Whisk the hot cocoa mixture into dry ingredients. Stir in the sour cream mixture just to combine; don't overmix. Scrape the batter into the prepared pan and bake until a toothpick inserted in the center of the cake comes out clean, about 35 minutes.

4. Cool the cake on a rack for 15 minutes, then unmold, turn it upright, and cool completely on the rack. Dust with confectioners' sugar and serve with ice cream or whipped cream, if desired.

COOK'S NOTE We prefer Dutch-process cocoa here over natural cocoa for its fuller, deeper flavor.

- pantry picks
- double duty
- real quick
- cool tools

Prep time: 30 minutes

It may not be polite to stare, but yes, these pears taste just as good as they look.

brown sugar-glazed pears
4 servings

PEARS

- 2 tablespoons unsalted butter
- 1/3 cup firmly packed dark brown sugar
- 4 Bartlett pears, peeled, cored, and halved lengthwise
- 1 tablespoon freshly squeezed lemon juice
- 1/2 teaspoon pure vanilla extract
- 1/8 teaspoon almond extract (optional)
- Gingery Mascarpone (see recipe, below) or whipped cream cheese
- Toasted slivered almonds

MASCARPONE

Makes 1 cup

- 1/2 cup mascarpone cheese
- 1/4 cup confectioners' sugar
- 1/3 cup chilled heavy cream
- 1 teaspoon freshly grated ginger
- 1/2 teaspoon pure vanilla extract
- Few drops mint extract

1. Position an oven rack about 6 inches from the broiler and preheat to high. Melt the butter in an ovenproof skillet just large enough to hold the pears in one layer. Crumble the brown sugar into the skillet and add the pears cut side down. Cook until the sugar begins to melt and the pears get juicy. Turn the pears with a wooden spoon or heatproof spatula to coat evenly with the melted sugar, then position them cut side down in the pan and transfer the skillet to the oven. Broil the pears, swirling the pan occasionally and turning the pears once, until they are brown on both sides and the sugar begins to caramelize, about 10 minutes in all.

2. Using a slotted spoon, transfer 2 pear halves to each of 4 small plates. Whisk the lemon juice, vanilla, and almond extract, if using, into the skillet until smooth. Spoon this sauce around and on top of the pears. Spoon a dollop of Gingery Mascarpone or whipped cream cheese next to the pears and scatter some nuts over the tops.

GINGERY MASCARPONE

Lightly blend the mascarpone and sugar in a bowl. Beat the cream to soft peaks in another bowl with the grated ginger, vanilla extract, and mint extract. Gently fold the mixture into the mascarpone.

SHOPSMART When buying pears, remember your ABCs—Anjou, Bartlett, and Comice. For baking, they're the tastiest and juiciest.

chocolate malted panna cotta
4 servings

Our playful panna cotta will comfort the worldliest of souls and put you at ease when dessert time comes.

2 tablespoons cold water

1 teaspoon pure vanilla extract

2½ teaspoons unflavored gelatin

2 cups heavy cream

½ cup chocolate malted milk powder

⅓ cup sugar

1 or 2 bananas, peeled

Hot Fudge Sauce (see recipe, page 193) and sweetened whipped cream, for serving (optional)

1. Put the cold water and vanilla in a small bowl and sprinkle the gelatin over the top. Set aside.

2. Put the cream, chocolate malted milk powder, and sugar in a medium saucepan and bring to a boil over high heat, stirring occasionally. Pull the pan from the heat and whisk in the gelatin mixture until dissolved. Divide among four 8-ounce paper cups and freeze until set, about 2 hours.

3. To serve, peel off the paper and invert the panna cotta onto individual dessert plates. Thinly slice the banana or bananas (use 2 bananas if cutting lengthwise) and arrange slices or halves around each panna cotta. Serve with a drizzle of Hot Fudge Sauce and a dollop of whipped cream, if desired.

STYLE No more struggling with ramekins. We set our panna cotta up in paper cups instead. Gently tear the cups away and flip the desserts out onto pretty plates for a clean finish.

● pantry picks
● *freezer duty*
● *marinades*
● *cool tools*

**Prep time: 20 minutes active time
(1 hour in the refrigerator)**

This classic *dolce* has graced every trattoria menu since the '80s. This new *rapido* version made us fall for it all over again.

tiramisù rapido
4 servings

¼ cup coffee liqueur

¼ cup water

2 tablespoons espresso powder

6 tablespoons confectioners' sugar

8 ladyfingers

8 ounces mascarpone cheese

½ cup heavy cream

2 teaspoons ground chocolate or sweetened cocoa

1. Whisk the coffee liqueur, water, espresso powder, and 2 tablespoons of the confectioners' sugar in a glass measuring cup until smooth. Pour about ⅓ cup of the mixture over the ladyfingers in a shallow bowl, then toss and set aside.

2. Gently beat with a handheld mixer the remaining espresso mixture and the remaining 4 tablespoons confectioners' sugar into the mascarpone until smooth. Take care not to overbeat it or the mascarpone will be grainy. Using the same beaters (no need to clean them), beat the whipped cream to soft peaks and fold it into the mascarpone mixture.

3. To assemble the tiramisù: Crumble half the soaked ladyfingers into four 8-ounce parfait or wine glasses. Spoon ¼ cup of the mascarpone mixture over the ladyfingers and press and spread gently with the back of the spoon to fill the spaces between the ladyfinger pieces. Repeat with remaining ladyfingers and mascarpone mixture. Sprinkle ½ teaspoon ground chocolate over each tiramisù, cover with plastic wrap, and refrigerate for at least 1 hour or overnight before serving.

COOK'S NOTE Ladyfingers are little oblong sponge cakes that look like wide fingers. We prefer the crisp Italian *savoyardi* variety to the soft sponge-cake type.

the simplified kitchen

Follow our tips for stocking your pantry, shopping smart, and using cool tools. You'll be cooking great food fast and easily in no time.

Stock your pantry.

When it's time to get cooking, the pantry is often our starting place. A well-stocked pantry (which includes the fridge, freezer, and cupboards) makes cooking a breeze.

Your pantry should reflect your taste. If the cupboard's bare and you are starting from scratch, build your pantry gradually. Begin with essentials, and then add some of your favorite fun ingredients as your recipe repertoire expands.

IN THE CUPBOARD

Oil: Extra-virgin olive and a neutral oil such as soy, corn, vegetable, or peanut
Vinegar: Balsamic, red, and white wine
Broth: Low-sodium chicken, beef, and a vegetable broth such as mushroom if you're a vegetarian
Noodles & grains: A selection of pasta shapes and Asian-style noodles such as soba, quick-cooking polenta, grits, and bulgur
Vegetables: Canned tomatoes, whole and crushed; sun-dried tomatoes; tomato paste (we love the paste in tubes); roasted peppers; pepperoncini; marinated artichokes; dried or canned mushrooms
Fruit: Dried fruits such as apricots, cherries, cranberries, and currants; applesauce
Spreads: Olive or tomato tapenade, pestos, peanut butter
Beans, canned: Black, cannellini, chickpeas, and kidney
Crackers & coatings: Graham crackers, saltines, plain bread crumbs, panko (coarse Japanese bread crumbs), cornstarch

UNDER THE COUNTER

Garlic & onions: red, white, and yellow onions; shallots
Potatoes: Russet, red, yellow-fleshed

ON THE SPICE RACK

Kosher salt and black peppercorns for your mill
Bay leaves

Dried thyme
Crushed red pepper or cayenne pepper
Cinnamon
Whole nutmeg
Dried oregano
Cumin
Coriander
Dried mint
Dried sage
Onion powder
Garlic powder
Ground ginger
Saffron
Herb and spice blends, such as chili powder, curry, herbes de Provence, and Chinese five-spice powder

FOR BAKING

All-purpose flour
Baking powder and baking soda
Sugar (granulated, confectioners', light or dark brown), honey, and light corn syrup
Vanilla extract
Chocolate chips, Dutch-process cocoa, semisweet bars
Coffee or espresso powder
Condensed milk
Gelatin

IN THE FRIDGE

Eggs
Milk
Unsalted butter
Mustard
Fresh herbs
A favorite cheese
Olives
Lemons, oranges, and limes
Scallions
Ginger
Half-and-half or heavy cream

Sour cream
Hot sauce
Horseradish
Chutney and relishes
Jellies and jams (red currant, apricot, raspberry)

IN THE FREEZER

Ice cream
Nuts (they stay fresh in the freezer)
Spinach
Strawberries and other bagged fruits
Raw peeled and deveined shrimp
Juice concentrates
Puff pastry

flavor fast

Ethnic accents lend a fresh twist to any meal. Start with a small collection of your favorite ethnic flavorings, then add new things as you discover them.

Asian Accents

Soy sauce
Dark sesame oil
Miso paste (fermented soybeans)
Coconut milk
Rice vinegar
Shaohsing rice cooking wine or pale dry sherry
Southeast Asian fish sauce
Thai curry paste
Wasabi (Japanese horseradish)

South-of-the-Border Flair

Jarred tomato or tomatillo salsa
Chipotle chiles *en adobo* (smoked and dried jalapeños packed in sauce)
Pickled jalapeños
Tortilla chips

Be a smart shopper. Smart shopping is more than just clipping coupons. Smart shoppers go into their grocery stores with a game plan and know how to pick out the best fish, meats, and cheeses. Learn what we've learned about how to make your market work for you.

SPEED SHOPPING

• Save time by keeping a grocery list of standard weekly purchases—such as eggs, milk, deli meats, and vegetables—on your computer. Print, take inventory, and go.

• Organize your list by supermarket sections, placing vegetables together, dairy items together, etc., so you can shop efficiently.

• Shop from the back of the market to the front for a straight path to the checkout line.

• Program your supermarket's phone number into your cell phone. When you can't find an item, it can be faster to call than to track down someone who can help. Call ahead to preorder roasts or special-order meats or fish.

BUYING GUIDE

DAIRY

Eggs: Open cartons to make sure eggs are crack-free. Store in the carton or a sealed container—not in the door of your fridge, where they absorb odors.

Butter: Store in a butter dish. Keep one stick of butter in the fridge at a time; freeze the rest for optimal freshness. Keep butter away from any strongly flavored items such as garlic or cheese.

Milk: Reach for the milk cartons in the back of the dairy case; these are usually the freshest and have the latest expiration date.

Cheeses: Wrap hard cheese, such as Parmesan and pecorino, in parchment or waxed paper and then in plastic wrap or a resealable plastic bag. Medium-

what kind of shopper are you?

If you're an express-lane shopper (you stop in the market a couple of times a week): Shop for pantry items such as rice, olive oil, and pasta in bulk once a month. During the week, grab fresh items and go.

If you're a once-a-week shopper: Use perishable groceries such as asparagus, basil, and fish early on in the week; use the hardier foods such as root vegetables, broccoli, eggs, and roasts later on in the week.

hard cheese, such as cheddar, Jack, and mozzarella, can be bundled in plastic wrap. Wrap soft cheese, such as fresh goat or Brie, in plastic to cover the exposed surface or interior, then put in a resealable plastic bag.

POULTRY & MEAT

The freshest meat:
• Poultry is plump and moist.
• Red meat has a rosy cast.
• Packages are well sealed and not moist or leaking.
• Freshness dates have not expired.
• Raw meats should be kept separate from produce in your cart.

Roasts Defined
Beef chuck roast: Sometimes called a blade roast, top blade roast, or pot roast. It's flavorful, juicy, and tender.
Beef brisket: The point cut is more flavorful than the flat cut.
Beef shins: Also called shanks or crosscut shanks. The bones add a big, beefy flavor to round out sauces and stews; the meat is melt-in-your-mouth tender.
Pork blade roast: From the shoulder or shoulder end of a loin. These cook up tender, juicy, and flavorful. Alternatives: Boston butt and picnic shoulders.
When you get home : Store meats in the coolest spot of the fridge—lower shelves near the back are often best. Ground meat keeps for 2 days; poultry for 2 days; beef and pork roasts and chops for 3 to 5 days.

FISH

The freshest fish:
• Smells fresh, not fishy.
• Filets look moist and pristine with no gaps between the muscles.
• Whole are shiny with clear eyes, as if just pulled from the sea.

SHELLFISH

Shrimp: Don't be afraid of frozen shrimp. Most "fresh" shrimp in markets have been frozen and are simply defrosted. Frozen peeled and deveined shrimp are so convenient and great to have in your freezer. Check the numbers on the bags to know the shrimp size—for example, "16/20" means extra-large shrimp with 16 to 20 shrimp per pound; the higher the numbers, the smaller the shrimp. Defrost shrimp in a bowl of cold water for about 20 minutes.
Scallops: Ask for "dry" untreated scallops, (scallops can be soaked in a chemical solution to extend their shelf life); they cook and taste better. Treated scallops look snow-white.
Mussels and clams: Look for closed shells or those that close when tapped.
When you get home: Keep seafood well chilled. Fill a resealable plastic bag with ice and lay fish or shellfish on top. Open plastic bags of mussels and clams.

VEGETABLES

Stay-fresh tips:
• Buy carrots and beets with their tops attached—they're sweeter. Remove tops at home to keep them crisp.
• Remove bands and ties from vegetables and herbs; if stored in a tight bunch, they can deteriorate.
• Store hardy herbs such as rosemary and thyme in a paper towel-lined container. Store herbs with roots still attached, such as basil and cilantro, in water covered with a plastic bag.
• Tuck asparagus, celery, fennel, leeks, and zucchini into sealed plastic bags.
• Place broccoli, carrots, cauliflower, and eggplant in perforated bags for best storage.
• Repack mushrooms in a paper bag or bowl covered with a paper towel.
• Store salad greens in a salad spinner lined with paper towels or in a large sealed plastic container.
• Don't refrigerate tomatoes! Store them, uncovered, at room temperature.

fish types

Fish comes in three categories: oily, flaky, and meaty. Look for the freshest specimen in a category rather than for a specific variety.

Fish in the same category cook in about the same time. Swap one for another within those categories.

Flaky White Fish
Cod
Flounder
Grouper
Orange roughy
Skate

Oily Fish
Bluefish
Catfish
Red mullet
Red snapper
Sea bass
Trout

Meaty Fish
Arctic char
Halibut
Salmon
Swordfish
Tuna

Use cool tools. Kitchen accoutrements help make cooking fast and easy. Here's how to use some of our favorite tools.

SLOW COOKERS

Deep, meaty flavors once possible only through long, slow stove top braising are both attainable and virtually effortless when you use a slow cooker. The best part is you don't even need to be home while it's working its magic.

SLOW COOKER BASICS

How it works: A slow cooker provides low, even heat that gently cooks food over many hours. The temperature of cooking ranges from 200°F to 300°F.

Safety first!: Because the slow cooker cooks food at a low temperature for a long time, it's important to make sure that your slow cooker heats food to a hot enough, safe temperature. To test your slow cooker, place 2 quarts of water in the bowl and cook on low 8 hours. Lift the lid and check the water's temperature—if it doesn't read at least 185°F, it's time for a new cooker.

TIPS FOR SLOW COOKING

• Inexpensive cuts of meat that become more tender as they cook work best. For the leanest slow-cooked meals, remember to trim the fat off meat before browning or adding to the slow cooker.

• For extra layers of flavor, brown meat and vegetables in separate pans, then transfer items to your slow cooker along with those delicious pan drippings. Add fresh herbs, citrus, vinegar, or spices at the end for a bright finish.

• Avoid slow cooking chicken or turkey. Because it can take up to 4 hours for the items in a slow cooker to come to a boil, we avoid ingredients that are food safety risks.

SLOW COOKER TECHNIQUE

• When converting a recipe, reduce the amount of liquid called for. Sauces don't thicken as much because the slow cooker doesn't cook food at an intense simmer.

• Cut down on cayenne pepper—it intensifies in a slow cooker. Rosemary turns too piney if added at the very beginning of the cooking time. Steep it for just a minute or two at the end.

• Resist the temptation to peek! Removing the lid from a slow cooker releases valuable heat and can increase the cooking time by up to one hour. Spin the lid to remove condensation so you can see inside the pot.

• If you don't see condensation building beneath the slow cooker's lid, this means that the seal isn't tight. An easy solution is to place a damp towel over the pot, place the lid on the towel, and fold its ends over the lid.

• Prep your ingredients the night before so that the next morning you can throw everything in the pot and go. You can even brown meats the night before. Don't store the slow cooker bowl in the fridge, though—it will take too long for it to heat up to the proper temperature.

TIP: SLOW COOKER ALTITUDE ADJUSTMENT

If you live above 2,000 feet, add an hour or two as needed to the cooking time.

PRESSURE COOKERS

A pressure cooker cooks foods three times faster than cooking on the stove top. We love it for stews, soups, and risottos. Follow our tips and become a pressure cooking pro.

PRESSURE COOKER BASICS

How it works: When a pressure cooker is sealed and placed over heat, the simmering liquid in the pot builds up and produces 15 pounds of pressure. The 250°F (regular steam is 212°F) pressurized steam penetrates the food, cooking it three times as fast as normal.

Safety first!: Although today's pressure cookers are much safer and more dependable than the pressure cookers of yore, it's always smart to keep your safety on the front burner. Read your pressure cooker's manual. In it you'll find important information about how much food and liquid you can place in your pressure cooker, how to lock the lid, and how to safely release the pressure.

Additional safety tips

• Position steam vent away from you.

• After releasing the pressure, open the lid away from your face.

• Use an oven mitt or thick kitchen towel when removing the lid.

• Never open a pressure cooker before it finishes depressurizing.

TIPS FOR COOKING UNDER PRESSURE

• Boost flavor by taking time to brown your meat and vegetables first and adding fresh herbs, quick-cooking shrimp, or cheese at the end to heighten flavors.

• Keep your vegetables cut large. If they're too small, they'll disintegrate.

PRESSURE COOKER TECHNIQUE

• If converting a recipe from stove top to a pressure cooker, reduce the amount of liquid called for because liquid doesn't evaporate.

• Pay attention to the minimum and maximum marks inside your pressure cooker. Never fill your pressure cooker with too much food; this prevents steam from building inside the cooker.

• Add ingredients to the pot either at the beginning or stir in at the end after the pressure has been released from the pot. You can't add items throughout the cooking process—it's just too hot in there!

PRESSURE COOKER CARE

• Remove and clean the gasket and the rubber seal after each use and air dry before returning it to the lid. Keep the gasket supple by lightly coating it with vegetable oil before storing.

• Clean the vent/valve area while you're cleaning the lid. We like to use a toothbrush to get into tight spots.

• Test your pressure cooker's seal by placing 2 cups of water in it and bringing it up to pressure. If water drips down the sides of the pot or if it never comes up to pressure, it's time to buy a new gasket.

• Store your pressure cooker with the lid separate from the base so it can air out between uses.

TIP: PRESSURE COOKER ALTITUDE ADJUSTMENT

If you live more than 2,000 feet above sea level, increase the cooking time for pressure cooker recipes by 5 percent for every 1,000 feet above the 2,000-foot elevation.

more cool tools

Whether you're slow cooking, pressure cooking, or just cooking, here are a few of our favorite tools to help you cook efficiently.

Digital Thermometer:
Takes the guesswork out of cooking meat and poultry.

Microwave:
Makes quick chutneys and sauces, cooks vegetables, melts butter, makes hot fudge sauce, and reheats leftovers.

Blender & Immersion Blender:
Turn a chunky sauce or soup into a smooth one. An immersion (stick) blender does it right in the pan.

Minichopper & Food Processor:
Quickly make spice pastes, gremolatas, chutneys, and fresh salsas.

pressure cooker quick release

To bring the pressure down fast so food doesn't overcook, use the quick-release method. Just press down on the indicator stem until no more steam comes out. When the pressure indicator stem remains in its lowest position, all of the steam has been released.

index

221

index

223

index